WORLD WAR II
DESERT WAR

Stephen W. Sears

AMERICAN HERITAGE • NEW WORD CITY

Published by New Word City, Inc.

For more information about New Word City, visit our Web site at
NewWordCity.com

CHAPTER 1
DESERT BATTLEGROUND

Marshal Rodolfo Graziani, governor general of the colony of Libya, commander of the Italian 10th Army, was unhappy as he read his new orders. They came from Italy's head of state, Benito Mussolini, and they were blunt: Attack within two days or face dismissal. Graziani was an impressive figure, full-fleshed and handsome, with silver hair and a noble profile, but he was far less confident than he looked. He believed to attack now in the North African desert would be to court defeat, and defeat in the desert, he warned, would "inevitably develop into a rapid and total disaster."

As Graziani saw it that September day in 1940, Italy was not prepared for war, certainly not war in North Africa. He knew what desert fighting was like. Before

World War II, he had led a campaign to conquer the Senussi, a tribe of Arabs rebelling against Italian rule in Libya, and the experience had been a sobering one. The desert was barren, featureless, and all but waterless. The difficulties of keeping an army supplied were staggering. Desert fighting imposed its own special rules, which Graziani suspected his 10th Army had not yet learned.

All summer long he had been badgered to take the offensive. In June 1940, Mussolini dragged Italy into World War II to pick up the spoils of victory and revive the glories of ancient Rome. Egypt, with her fertile Nile delta, her storied cities of Alexandria and Cairo, her famous Suez Canal, seemed to promise both. Push aside the small British army stationed there, said il Duce, and the prize will fall like a ripe plum; Graziani had 250,000 soldiers in Libya, surely enough for the job. By July, Mussolini was writing Adolf Hitler, his fellow dictator in Germany, that "preparations for an attack on Egypt with vast objectives are now complete." As an observer remarked, "From a balcony in Rome, it looked easy."

Part of Graziani's reluctance to attack came from his cautious nature, part from shortages of the essentials of desert warfare (trucks, tanks, and antitank guns), and part from a healthy respect for his British opponents. While Mussolini harassed him from long distance, General Sir Archibald

Wavell's Western Desert Force snapped at him from close range.

Hardly had Italy declared war before fast-moving British columns of tanks, armored cars, and artillery seized the Italian forts guarding the Egyptian-Libyan frontier. A few days later, a well-armed Italian scouting force was ambushed and almost wiped out, losing seventeen tanks, a battery of field artillery, and some 100 men killed or captured; the British suffered no casualties at all. These hit-and-run raids continued through the summer. By September, Graziani had lost 3,500 men and Mussolini his patience. From Rome came the order to attack.

On September 13, 1940, Graziani's 10th Army heaved itself into motion at Sidi Omar, its advance base near the Egyptian frontier. For four days, it rumbled eastward along the coast road that runs parallel with the Mediterranean. Motorcyclists led the way, backed up by swarms of tanks and assault guns. Infantry followed in an endless procession of trucks. A small British rear guard fell back, persistently shelling the advancing Italians. At Sidi Barrani, a cluster of dusty, whitewashed mud huts sixty-five miles inside Egypt, Graziani halted and began building elaborate defenses. For the time being, at least, his offensive was over.

The 10th Army came to a stop on September 16. For nearly three months, it made no further threatening moves. Graziani busied himself digging his army into a chain of fortified desert camps that stretched fifty miles south from Sidi Barrani. General Wavell spent the three months stockpiling supplies and sharpening his plans.

Archibald Wavell was square-jawed and solidly built and every inch the professional soldier. As a young officer, he had served with the famous Black Watch in India; during World War I, he fought in France, where he lost an eye in combat, and in Palestine. Between wars, his military education included service with Britain's newly formed armored force. His lined face was usually expressionless, and his long silences were legendary throughout the British Army. But beneath this quiet mask was a man of great sensitivity and intelligence who wrote poetry to relax and who planned military operations with boldness and ingenuity. On August 2, 1939, he took command of the British Commonwealth forces in the Middle East. A month later, Nazi Germany's assault on Poland triggered World War II.

Wavell's Middle East command included Egypt, the Sudan, East Africa, and the oil-rich lands around the Persian Gulf - nine countries in all, with a total area of almost 3.5 million square miles. Some were British colonies; others, like Egypt, had signed treaties calling for protection by British forces. The Suez Canal was Britain's vital link to the Far East, but more important were the oil fields in Iraq and around the Persian Gulf upon which Britain's army, navy, and air force depended. Losing the Mediterranean and the Middle East would be a fatal blow to Great Britain's war effort.

Many people in the United States and Europe believed that Britain was doomed regardless of what happened in the Middle East. Her allies had collapsed one by one until she stood alone. In the spring of 1940, Hitler's blitzkrieg ("lightning war") engulfed Western Europe, defeating France and driving the British army on the Continent back across the English Channel. The British prepared for the invasion while their fighter pilots battled the German Air Force in the skies. As summer turned to fall, the threat of an assault lessened, but now the Luftwaffe's planes poured bombs into London and other cities almost nightly. Britons at home read of Graziani's army camped within striking distance of the Suez Canal and complained bitterly about the do-nothings at "Headquarters Muddle East."

Wavell's problems were many, large, and complex. His most pressing danger came from Graziani's 250,000 men at Sidi Barrani and in Libya, but there were another 350,000 Italian soldiers in East Africa to worry about. Wavell could count 86,000 troops throughout his entire Middle East command, most of them poorly equipped. He had kept Graziani at bay largely by a game of bluff. The trick, as a war correspondent described it, was to "make one man appear to be a dozen, make one tank look like a squadron, make a raid look like an advance." Finally, more tanks and guns and supplies arrived from England, and Wavell decided to stop bluffing and start fighting.

The Western Desert Force defending Egypt boasted two whole formations, the infantry of the 4th Indian Division and the Desert Rats of the 7th Armored Division, so called for the red jerboa, a small, rat-like desert creature, painted as an emblem on their vehicles. In charge of the two divisions was Lieutenant General Richard O'Connor, a slight, shy, quiet-spoken man who, like Wavell, had in him a streak of boldness and a talent for command.

In late October, Wavell directed Western Desert Force headquarters to prepare a plan for an offensive against the Italians at Sidi Barrani. Ten days later, O'Connor's plan was approved. Because Cairo, where Wavell had his headquarters, was thick with spies, only a handful of officers were told of the attack. O'Connor's army in the desert was sealed off by canceling all passes to Alexandria and Cairo. In the last week of November, a training exercise was held. The troops attacked dummy enemy camps that duplicated those of the Italians, which had been carefully photographed by planes of the Royal Air Force. O'Connor's offensive, codenamed Operation Compass, was to begin on December 7, 1940. On that day, to deceive enemy spies, Wavell appeared at the Cairo race track and hosted a dinner party for officers.

As Wavell played out his deception in Cairo, the army in the desert was stirring into action. "Just before dusk," wrote an officer of the 7th Armored Division, "we started the move forward. I can vividly remember watching the tanks ahead with their hulls hidden in drifting clouds of dust but with each turret standing out clear and black against the fading western sky, each with two muffled heads emerging and two pennants fluttering above from the wireless aerial. Late at night we halted for refueling and a few hours of sleep. . . . Daylight revealed a wonderful sight, the whole desert to the north covered with a mass of dispersed vehicles - tanks, trucks, and guns all moving westwards with long plumes of dust rolling out behind. . . ."

The advance continued through the day. At noon, an Italian reconnaissance plane was sighted, but it soared unconcerned overhead. That night, the Western Desert Force leaped forward again until it lay within a few miles of Nibeiwa, one of the fortified Italian camps. A raid by RAF planes drowned out the noise of the truck engines and the clanking of tank tracks. By dawn on December 9, all units were in position. At a few minutes after 7:00 a.m., the British artillery opened up on Nibeiwa.

In terms of total manpower available to the two commanders, Graziani had an edge over

O'Connor of ten to one. However, in the vicinity of Sidi Barrani, the Italians had only 120 tanks while their attackers possessed 275. More significant, O'Connor had achieved complete surprise. He had penetrated a fifteen-mile gap between two Italian camps without being seen, putting his whole force in the middle of the enemy position.

The British shells falling into Nibeiwa had the same effect as kicking an anthill. Soldiers rushed out of their tents in every direction. The crewmen of an armored battalion were warming up their tank engines and eating their breakfasts when the blow fell. In ten minutes, most of them were casualties and all twenty-three of their tanks were wrecked.

O'Connor's force barged into the camp, led by its massive, slow-moving infantry tanks (called Matildas for their waddling, waltzing gait, like "Waltzing Matilda" in the song popular among Australian troops in the army). Trotting along behind the tanks came Indian infantrymen with fixed bayonets. The Italians fought fiercely, but their bullets and hand grenades bounced harmlessly off the thick, armored hides of the Matildas.

Within two hours, the British seized the camp. Some 2,000 prisoners were taken. The victors gorged themselves on fresh bread, vegetables, canned ham, and wine - Graziani's Italians were the best-provisioned army that fought in the desert war - then pressed northward through a sandstorm that covered the battlefield like a yellow fog. Graziani's entire front was shattered by nightfall.

The next day, the rest of the Italian camps were overrun or abandoned. Prisoners were taken faster than they could be counted. A British officer at Sidi Barrani radioed headquarters that his men were guarding "about five acres of officers and 200 acres of other ranks." War correspondent Alan Moorehead reported standing on the coast road and watching prisoners march eastward on either side of the road in columns that stretched from horizon to horizon. By December 12, three days after the fighting began, the only Italians left in Egypt were prisoners of war.

O'Connor pushed his men hard, using captured Italian trucks, gasoline, and food to keep moving as the troops outran their own supply lines. When four of Graziani's divisions withdrew into Bardia, a small port in Libya a few miles from the frontier, British armored forces swiftly reached around to cut the coast road behind them. Wavell sent the 6th Australian Division to relieve the Indian infantry and lay siege to Bardia.

The Italian position was strong, with steel and concrete gun emplacements, thickly sown fields of explosive land mines, coils of barbed wire, and wide, steep-sided ditches to block tanks. On January 3, 1941, the Australians attacked. The infantry cleared the way for the tanks, reducing the strong points and filling in the antitank ditches. Then the Matildas moved in to complete the breach. Three Royal Navy battleships added a hail of fifteen-inch shells to the assault. The next day, the tanks advanced into Bardia itself. The Italians fought on until January 5 when the last resistance was overcome. In Bardia that night, correspondent Moorehead watched as "prisoners swarmed in every direction, and even in the light of the fires which were licking up the white walls of the houses it was impossible to distinguish enemy from friend. All they wanted was food, shelter from fighting, and a guarantee of life."

The spoils included 40,000 prisoners, 462 artillery pieces, 127 tanks, and more than 700 trucks. However, the commander of the garrison, General Annibale Bergonzoli, was nowhere to be found. Bergonzoli was called Electric Whiskers by his troops, who insisted that his bristling red beard gave off sparks. The Aussies resolved to catch Electric Whiskers and see this display for themselves.

Under O'Connor's prodding, the Desert Rats of the 7th Armored Division thrust westward again and cut off the Italian garrison at Tobruk, seventy miles beyond Bardia. Once more the Australians began to lay siege. They broke through the defenses on January 21, and Tobruk surrendered the next day. A mountain of supplies was seized, and the number of prisoners came to 25,000. Victorious

Australians wandered through the town wearing swords and medals taken from Italian officers, gorging themselves on canned fruit, and lighting their cigarettes with Italian money. But Electric Whiskers again slipped away.

After Tobruk's fall, Marshal Graziani gave up hope of holding Cyrenaica, the northeastern part of Libya bulging out into the Mediterranean. As he had predicted, defeat had turned into disaster. His army proved as ponderous and slow moving as a dinosaur, unable to react to the swift slashes of its enemy. His tanks were outgunned and his generals outthought. Against O'Connor's driving leadership and well-trained desert fighters, the bravery of individual Italian soldiers went for nothing.

Graziani's 10th Army retreated as fast as it could, mining the coast road behind it. Western Desert Force limped along in pursuit in a patchwork of battered vehicles, many of them captured and running on Italian gasoline. Both armies suffered equally from thirst and exhaustion.

At Mechili, 100 miles west of Tobruk, O'Connor put everything into one final thrust to achieve victory. The Desert Rats were down to fifty cruiser tanks - faster and lighter than the Matildas and intended for tank versus tank fighting - and ninety-five light tanks armed only with machine guns. Their other vehicles were falling apart, and their supply situation was a shambles.

Nevertheless, O'Connor sent the 7th Armored on a shortcut through the unmapped desert toward the coast road south of Benghazi to prevent the Italian retreat. The Australians would continue to pursue Electric Whiskers along the coast road and threaten Benghazi from the north.

On February 4, the Desert Rats and their bantam-sized Irish commander, Michael O'Moore Creagh, set off on the adventure. They immediately hit the worst going yet in the desert, a fifty-mile stretch of rock outcropping that chewed up tires and broke tank tracks. Soon the desert was littered with broken-down vehicles stripped of supplies, and drained of gas, and abandoned. When RAF reconnaissance planes reported that convoys of Italian trucks were beginning to head south from Benghazi, General Creagh assembled "Combeforce," a small, fast unit of trucks, guns, and armored cars under Lieutenant Colonel John Combe, to hurry ahead and block the coast road. Combeforce set out at top speed at dawn on February 5; by noon, it had reached the road near Beda Fomm. Within thirty minutes, an Italian truck convoy from Benghazi ran into the ambush. O'Connor had won.

Meanwhile, Creagh's cruiser tanks were careening recklessly over the rough terrain at top speed to back up Combeforce with firepower. They reached the road at dusk and quickly became embroiled with Italian tanks in a sharp battle fought by the light of burning vehicles.

Throughout the next day, the hard fighting continued in a driving rain. Vehicles by the hundreds piled up against the British roadblocks. Tanks and antitank guns dueled at point-blank range as the Italians desperately tried to break through. The few that did were picked off by Combeforce, lying in wait a few miles to the south.

On February 7, the same day the Australians broke into Benghazi from the north, the Battle of Beda Fomm ended. A war correspondent with the Desert Rats found the battlefield "strewn with broken and abandoned equipment, tattered uniforms, piles of empty shell, and cartridge cases . . . littered with paper, rifles, and bedding. Here and there small groups of men tended the wounded who had been gathered together. Others were collecting and burying the dead. . . . Some equipment was still burning furiously."

More than 25,000 Italian soldiers and equipment of every kind were captured at Beda Fomm and Benghazi, and this time Electric Whiskers did not escape. An armored car overtook him as he drove out of Benghazi. "You got here a bit too quickly today," Bergonzoli admitted to his captors. Much to the disappointment of the Australians, he was hustled off to Cairo before they could test his famous beard.

In two months, O'Connor had advanced 500 miles and conquered all of Cyrenaica. With a force never larger than 30,000 men, he had taken 130,000 prisoners, 380 tanks, and almost 850 pieces of field artillery. His total casualties came to just over 1,900 killed, wounded, and captured. Operation Compass was one of the most startling triumphs of World War II, and the victory-starved British people greeted the news jubilantly.

O'Connor and Wavell quickly turned their thoughts to Tripoli, 500 miles to the west, Mussolini's last stronghold in North Africa. In London, however, the government of Prime Minister Winston Churchill had different plans. It decided it must honor a pledge to come to the aid of Greece, then teetering on the edge of war with Germany.

Western Desert Force was stripped to the bone to strengthen the Greeks. Wavell considered this move an acceptable risk, for he believed Graziani's army was too badly mauled to pose much of a threat. He also had to keep up the pressure on the Italian army in East Africa. As soon as the campaigns in Greece and East Africa were over, he could rebuild the desert army and advance on Tripoli.

On February 12, 1941, five days after the Battle of Beda Fomm, Lieutenant General Erwin Rommel of the German Army stepped off a plane at Tripoli. Adolf Hitler had decided to shore up his floundering Italian ally, and General Rommel was his choice to command the German units on their way to North Africa. Two days after his arrival, Rommel wrote his wife: "All going as well as I could wish. I hope to be able to pull it off. . . ."

CHAPTER 2
ROMMEL TO THE RESCUE

Those who fought in the Western Desert and those who reported the fighting there devoted a good deal of effort to describing the setting. They noted the daytime heat and the nighttime cold, the swarming flies and the gritty, blowing sand, the spectacular sunsets and the star-filled night skies. And As they groped for a proper descriptive image, the one they most often hit upon was to compare the desert to the ocean.

Often, nothing but the unbroken line of the horizon could be seen in any direction. Vehicles moved freely across this expanse like ships at sea. Men did not just drive in the desert, they navigated, getting where they wanted to go by using speedometer, and map, and compass. The few landmarks were usually man-made: a heap of rocks or empty gasoline cans, a stone cistern for catching rainwater, a whitewashed Moslem mosque, a long procession of telephone poles. The only paved road was the coast road. Inland, vehicles followed rough, dusty tracks that avoided the worst of the rocky outcroppings and patches of soft sand.

From the shore of the Mediterranean, the Libyan Desert, or the Western Desert, as it was called in those days, climbs upward in a haphazard series of steps, or escarpments. In most places, these escarpments are too steep for trucks and even for tanks, so the few natural gaps, or passes, became important military objectives. The surface of the desert is largely underlaid with limestone; tracked vehicles, at least, could drive almost anywhere on it. Only well inland does the true desert of drifting sand dunes begin. Narrow, stony ravines, called wadies, look from the air like jagged cracks. Here and there are lie large dish-like depressions known as deirs. Inland from the sea, rain falls only two or three times a year - and in some places, only once in two or three years.

A German general aptly described North Africa as a "tactician's paradise and a quartermaster's hell." The long, narrow desert battlefield stretched over 1,400 miles from Tripoli on the west, the Axis' major port, to Alexandria on the east, the Allies' chief base. The Germans and the Italians on the one hand and the British on the other were willing to spend their blood and treasure to win this desolate strip of land simply because neither side could afford to let the other have it. For the British, the Western Desert was the buffer that protected the Suez Canal and the Middle Eastern oil fields, both of which the Axis powers wanted. In addition, whoever controlled the North African airfields was well ahead in the race to control the strategically vital Mediterranean.

As Marshal Graziani had ruefully noted, desert war imposed its own special rules. Rule number one was that armies brought with them everything they needed. There was no way to live off the country. As a result, the two most precious liquids were gasoline and water. For the British soldier, remarked a war correspondent, "The great problem in the mornings was to decide whether to make tea with the shaving water or to shave in the tea." What was left of a man's daily water ration (seldom more than a gallon) after drinking, cooking, bathing, and washing his clothes had to go into the radiator of his vehicle.

The second rule was the importance of complete mobility. In the desert, infantrymen did not march; they rode in trucks. The queen of battle was the tank. Closely related to mobility was rule number three: the need for speed. A fast-moving, quick-off-the-mark army, as General O'Connor's

Western Desert Force had proved, possessed an enormous edge, and a quick-thinking, energetic general could dominate an opponent who paused to gather up all the loose ends.

The final rule of desert warfare dealt with the nature of the battlefield itself. There were no industrial centers to capture, no captive populations to rule, no political considerations to clutter up tactics. It was a purely military struggle on an empty stage, and it was entirely possible to honor whatever "rules of the game" might still exist in a total war.

To meet the pressing needs in Greece and East Africa, General Wavell had left the Western Desert Force gravely weakened. "Next month or two will be anxious," he cabled Prime Minister Churchill in March 1941, but he estimated that the enemy in Libya would not be strong enough to risk an attack before May. This, in fact, was precisely the timetable given in Hitler's orders to General Rommel. The turn of events was to surprise Hitler as much as Wavell.

Erwin Rommel was a forty-nine-year-old professional soldier whose reckless bravery during World War I had brought him two wounds and the Pour le Mérite, Germany's highest military decoration. Outspoken and blunt, Rommel lacked the arrogant polish of the Prussian aristocracy that supplied the German Army with so many of its officers. In the 1930s, a book he wrote stressing boldness in infantry tactics caught Adolf Hitler's eye. In 1940, during the Battle of France, he led a panzer division with dash and brilliance. Hitler concluded that here was the man to come to the aid of Mussolini. The moment Rommel set foot in North Africa, the situation began to happen.

Hitler had promised Mussolini an "Afrika Korps" of two German divisions, one armored and one of motorized infantry. When the 5th Light Motorized Division - a self-contained force of infantry, armor, artillery, and antitank and antiaircraft guns - arrived at Tripoli in February 1941, Rommel ordered the ships unloaded through the night, ignoring the danger of the RAF bombing the lighted docks. He put his engineers to building dummy wooden tanks atop little Volkswagen staff cars to make the British think he was stronger than he was, and he hurried his advance units to El Agheila, the westernmost British outpost in Libya, to test the enemy's strength.

The army that faced Rommel was not the same fast-moving, quick-thinking force that had chased Marshal Graziani out of Egypt. The Desert Rats of the 7th Armored Division, back in Egypt for rest and refitting, had been replaced by the newly arrived 2nd Armored Division, green and at half strength. The 6th Australian Infantry, victors at Bardia and Tobruk and Benghazi, was relieved by another Australian division, untrained and poorly equipped. Replacing O'Connor in command was Lieutenant General Philip Neame, a newcomer to the desert.

On March 24, 1941, the German advance guard drove the British out of El Agheila. A week later, Rommel launched a second attack. Sensing the weakness before him, he disregarded his orders. "It was a chance I could not resist," he wrote. By April 2, Neame's defenses were splintered. Orders went out to abandon Benghazi if necessary. Wavell commanded General O'Connor to fly at once to Cyrenaica to try to restore a defensive front.

There was little O'Connor could do, for Western Desert Force was rapidly falling apart. Communications broke down, orders were bungled, and troops went astray. An enormous supply dump containing most of the 2nd Armored's gas was set afire by its guards when they thought the enemy was approaching; the "enemy" turned out to be a British patrol.

As O'Connor had done earlier in the year, Rommel took the desert shortcut across the base of the Cyrenaican "bulge." He pushed his men relentlessly, flying from one column to another in his tiny Storch plane. When told that the vehicles needed servicing and repairs, he ordered his officers not to bother with such "trifles." The 5th Light Division's commander asked for a four-day halt to bring up ammunition and gasoline; Rommel had him empty all his trucks - leaving the division stranded immobile in the desert for twenty-four hours - and send them back to depots to bring up the needed supplies. An Italian general complained that he was being ordered into impassable terrain; Rommel drove ahead a dozen miles by himself to prove the path was clear.

Late on April 3, Rommel paused long enough to write his wife: "We've been attacking since the 31st with dazzling success. There'll be consternation amongst our masters in Tripoli and Rome and perhaps in Berlin, too. I took the risk against all orders and instructions because the opportunity seemed favorable. . . . You will understand that I can't sleep for happiness." By April 6, most of the Cyrenaican bulge was in Axis hands. Benghazi had fallen, and the spread fingers of Rommel's columns were reaching for Mechili, where the exhausted British were regrouping.

That night, a British staff car drove headlong into a German scouting force on one of the desert tracks north of Mechili. There was a brief exchange of gunfire, killing the British driver and a German motorcyclist. The staff car was surrounded, and the occupants were ordered to surrender. Out stepped generals Neame and O'Connor and Brigadier John Combe, whose Combeforce had slammed the door on the retreating Italians barely two months before. (So seriously did Wavell feel O'Connor's loss that he tried – unsuccessfully - to exchange him for any six captured Italian generals that Mussolini's high command cared to choose.)

The next day Mechili capitulated. The British streamed eastward. Most of the Australian infantry reached safety in the defenses of Tobruk, but the 2nd Armored Division was shattered; it never again appeared on the battle roles of the British Army. Seeking a quick victory, Rommel threw his troops at Tobruk. But his planning was too hurried and his men too exhausted, and the assault was repulsed. German armored forces bypassed the fortress and seized Bardia and Sallum, key points along the coastal escarpment. Cyrenaica had been regained, and once more the Axis were at the gates of Egypt.

April 1941 was a month of severe trial for Great Britain. Only the campaign against the Italians in East Africa went well. Officials in London sugar-coated the defeat in the Western Desert with such phrases as "a withdrawal to a battleground of our own choosing" and "part of a plan for an elastic defence," but few Britons were fooled. On April 6, Hitler attacked Yugoslavia, whose capital, Belgrade, fell within a week. Greece, too, was invaded. The forces sent there at such cost by Wavell could not stem the Nazi tide, and by the end of the month, they had to be evacuated. The British island of Malta, key to control of the Mediterranean, was savagely pounded by the Luftwaffe. Oil-rich Iraq, east of Suez, was torn by an anti-British revolt, and there were signs that a similar uprising was brewing in Syria. In a grim mood, Churchill wrote President Franklin D. Roosevelt: "In this war, every post is a winning-post, and how many more are we going to lose?"

As usual, Churchill met trouble by bounding into action. Axis submarines, warships, and planes were so thick in the Mediterranean that British ships carrying supplies to the Middle East took the slow, 14,000-mile route around Africa and through the Red Sea to Egypt. Now, overriding the objections of his military advisers, Churchill ordered the Royal Navy to force a passage through the Mediterranean with a convoy of merchant ships carrying tanks to General Wavell. The codename for his bold plan was Operation Tiger.

It would have comforted the prime minister to know that just then all was not serene in the Axis camp. Rommel was determined to press into Egypt and beyond as soon as he was re-supplied and the Tobruk thorn was removed from his flank. But his unexpected victories had embarrassed the German high command. because it had not intended North Africa to be a major theater of war. General Franz Halder, chief of the German General Staff, complained in his diary that Rommel did not even submit proper reports; instead, "All day long he rushes about between his widely scattered units." Something must be done to "head off this soldier gone stark mad," Halder thought, or he would embroil Germany in a campaign beyond her resources.

Shrugging off his first repulse at Tobruk, Rommel searched for a soft spot in its defenses. Tobruk was important because of its harbor, the only one of any size between Alexandria and Benghazi. The desert around the small, whitewashed town was flat as a plate; the verdict of one observer was that it "must have been difficult to defend even in the days of bows and arrows." Yet, before the war, the Italians had lavished tons of concrete and steel on its defenses.

A double row of strong points and trenches formed a semicircle thirty miles around the harbor. The British strengthened this line with barbed wire, tank traps, minefields, and a heavy concentration of artillery. The garrison, made up mostly of Australian infantry supported by a few tanks, was led by General Leslie Morshead. He and his Aussies were very and determined. "There is to be no surrender and no retreat," Morshead told his officers.

Rommel ordered three major assaults against the Australians, using a variety of tactics. But his forces were too weak, and the opposition too determined unwavering, to achieve a breakthrough. By May, he had to content himself with tightening the ring around the fortress while he waited impatiently for reinforcements.

The siege of Tobruk was to drag on for eight months, until the winter of 1941. It was a boring, bloody, dangerous stalemate for the men on both sides. They "went to ground" during the day, suffering the stifling heat and the swarming insects to avoid sniper's' bullets. Bombing and artillery fire took a steady toll. The desolate landscape, wrote a British war correspondent, was "littered with broken transport, burned-out tanks, and spent ammunition, as though some junk merchant had set up business on the surface of the moon." Morshead's garrison could be supplied only by ship and only at night, and British naval losses were heavy. But neither side would loosen its grip. To the British Commonwealth, Tobruk came to stand for stubborn courage in the face of adversity. To Rommel, Tobruk was a symbol of frustration. He vowed that the fortress would be his.

For General Wavell, events were fast rapidly reaching a climax. He moved his available forces across the vast chessboard of the Middle East - to put down revolts in Iraq and Syria, to gain final victory over the Italians in East Africa, to probe Rommel's outposts on the Egyptian frontier, to counter (unsuccessfully) a massive assault on the island of Crete by German paratroopers.

All the while a blizzard of telegrams from Churchill crying for action descended on Wavell's Cairo headquarters.

On May 12, 1941, the Tiger convoy anchored at Alexandria, having lost only one ship in the Mediterranean passage and bringing Wavell 238 tanks. Churchill, who had risked so much to get these reinforcements to the Middle East, waited anxiously for his Tiger Cubs, as he called them, to go into action. Wavell replied that Operation Battleaxe was scheduled for June 15. He intended to use the new tanks to break Rommel's shield at Sallum and Bardia and then advance seventy miles westward to lift the siege of Tobruk. The Desert Rats of the 7th Armored Division would spearhead the attack.

Battleaxe called for the 4th Indian Division, supported by infantry tanks, to capture Halfaya Pass, an important gap in the coastal escarpment near Sallum. The British armor would meanwhile swing around to the left beyond the Axis positions guarding Sallum and Bardia. Here, on the desert flank, Wavell saw the decisive tank battle taking place.

On the appointed morning, eighteen Matildas waddled toward Halfaya Pass, followed by Indian infantrymen in trucks. Before the tanks were close enough to fire effectively, they were hit by a hail of armor-piercing shells. Eleven of the twelve leading

Matildas stopped dead, some in flames, others with gun turrets blown completely off their hulls. Four others behind them withdrew, blundered into a mine field, and had tracks blown off. Later the same day, far out on the desert flank, a column of British cruiser tanks met the same devastating fire from a German strong point.

Thus were British armored forces introduced to the German eighty-eight-millimeter gun, one of the best artillery pieces of World War II. A dual-purpose antiaircraft and antitank gun, the long-barreled eighty-eight was accurate and fast firing, and its twenty-one-pound shell had tremendous hitting power; at a range of well over a mile, it could kill even the most heavily armored tank with a single shot. Rommel had only a dozen of these guns, but the five at Halfaya Pass had been dug into stony clefts so that the barrels were at ground level. In the shimmering desert haze and with their flash-less charges, they were all but invisible.

On the second day of Battleaxe, Rommel threw in the tanks of the 5th Light Division and the newly arrived 15th Panzer Division, the second of the two divisions Hitler had promised Mussolini. While neither side could claim a clear-cut advantage, Rommel was gaining the upper hand. Most of his outposts, including Halfaya Pass (by now, and ever after, known to the British as Hellfire Pass), had held firm. The 5th Light was on the flank of the Desert Rats, and the German armor was better concentrated. Most important, Rommel had found British field commanders cautious and unimaginative, and he was ready to seize the initiative. He would "deal the enemy an unexpected blow in his most sensitive spot" by a flank attack at first light on June 17 before the British could launch any attack of their own.

Rommel stayed a step ahead of his enemy. By four in the afternoon of June 17, his panzer columns hooked in toward Halfaya Pass while the British rushed eastward to escape encirclement. The British lost twenty-seven cruiser tanks and sixty-four Matildas - almost half their armored force. The Afrika Korps won the battlefield as well as the battle and recovered and repaired its damaged tanks; in all, Rommel lost only a dozen tanks.

The British concluded from the failure of Battleaxe that their tanks were outgunned by those of the enemy, which was not true. This error grew out of misunderstanding what had killed so many of their cruisers and Matildas. They believed German tanks were responsible, when, in most cases, the actual killers were antitank guns, particularly the eighty-eight. The failure to appreciate the full value of antitank guns, or how Rommel was using them, was to haunt the British in the months to come.

When the Battleaxe reports reached England,

Winston Churchill was at Chartwell, his country home, where he was awaiting the outcome. There he received news of the defeat. "A most bitter blow," he wrote, "I wandered about the valley disconsolately for some hours." Beyond the fact that his beloved Tiger Cubs had been so roughly handled was the grimmer realization that, for the first time, the desert army had struck a full-strength blow, only to be repulsed.

The Middle East needed new blood, Churchill thought. He had lost confidence in General Wavell. On June 21, he cabled Wavell that "the victories which are associated with your name will be famous in the story of the British Army," but that "the public interest will best be served" by a change in leadership. The new Middle East commander was to be General Sir Claude Auchinleck. Wavell would take Auchinleck's place as head of British Commonwealth forces in India.

Wavell received the news from an aide early the next morning in his Cairo home as he was shaving. He showed no emotion as he listened to the orders, remarked quietly "the Prime Minister's quite right - this job needs a new eye and a new hand," and went on shaving. He took his usual morning ride and swim and set about getting affairs in order for his successor.

For nearly two years, in victory and defeat, Archibald Wavell had kept the Middle East in the Allied column. Certainly no other British soldier in World War II shouldered so many burdens. He built the foundations for victories that other men would win. When the change of command was made public, correspondent Alan Moorehead wrote: "There went out of Cairo and the Middle East that afternoon one of the great men of the war."

Incident at Tobruk

During the eighth-month siege of Tobruk in 1941, the garrison averaged 23,000 fighting men, some 15,000 of them Australians. Their only link to the outside world was by sea. The RAF had to withdraw its fighters from Tobruk in the face of heavy Axis air attacks, leaving it unprotected, and hardly a day went by when there was not at least one raid. This is how one such raid by German dive bombers looked to an infantry platoon of the 9th Australian Division. It is from Eric Lambert's novel *The Twenty Thousand Thieves*; although it is fiction, it has the authentic ring of an eyewitness report.

> It was an ordinary Libyan day, furnace-hot with a glare that was like a knife across the eyes. Striking the stone-littered surface of the desert, the light quivered vaporously. The sky was the color of smoke. It was motionless. The sun was seen through it like a coin in a dim pool.
>
> But there was life in that sky.

Six Platoon sat in their pits. They were not the men who, attired correctly and uniformly, had marched around the roads of Palestine or stalked the streets of Jerusalem and Tel Aviv in quest of adventures. Their shorts were bleached to a dirty yellow and their boots were worn to whiteness by the sand. Gone was the slouch hat; in its place they wore the round steel helmet, painted yellow. Those who had discarded their shirts showed skins as brown as the wood in the butts of their rifles. Their eyes were keener, their faces leaner, their lips drawn finer. . . .

The whole platoon busied itself in a casual sort of fashion. Then, with one accord, they stopped and looked upwards. There was a faint pulsing in the sky . . . . The pulsing became a trembling, the trembling became a hum. Then suddenly the noise of the dive bombers burst out of the blue like a snarl.

"Here they are," cried Dick, and pointed to the east.

They came out of the sun, black and evil-looking Stukas. Their curiously shaped wings were like those of hawks, poised to drop on their prey. There were two flights of them. One flight peeled off, dwindling in the direction of the invisible town.

The world became all noise. Around them, the Bofors guns coughed out a torrent of explosions and the sky flowered with little white pom-poms of smoke. Farther back the heavy anti-aircraft brayed hideously upwards.

One by one the black shapes came earthwards, as if they hurtled down a gigantic slide. The shrieks of their downward passage pierced the sound of exploding bombs. The earth around the Australians vomited upwards in great black clouds.

The air became a fog of yellow dust and black smoke and through the frightful din came faintly the cries of men. . . .

Then, as suddenly as it began, the raid ceased. The anti-aircraft fire dwindled to isolated bangs. The noise of the Stukas grew fainter and fainter in the distance. Human voices carried through the drifting smoke. One of the voices called, high-pitched and urgent: "Stretcher-bearer!" Forms came running through the haze. . . .

Six Platoon came out of their pits to discover who were their latest casualties. Dick clambered across the parapet and made towards the wadi where men were already gathered. . . .

The two dead men had been placed on stretchers. Neither of them was well-known to Dick. One was a small grey man approaching middle age who had joined the battalion only a few days before it left Palestine. His remains formed an unnatural heap beneath a blanket through which the blood oozed. The other lay uncovered, his eyes looking sightlessly to the sky. None of Six Platoon had known him very well either. He had been a big, fair, smiling young fellow, always pleasant, but shy. All they knew about him was that he had been a motor mechanic and had a young wife to whom he wrote every day. He was not marked, but his clothes hung from him in a thousand small tatters where the blast had ripped across his body.

Watched by the men of Six Platoon, the stretcher-bearers bore the dead men slowly down the wadi. Andy gazed expressionlessly after them.

"That's that," he said.

CHAPTER 3
STRIKE AND
COUNTERSTRIKE

On June 22, 1941 - the same day that General Wavell learned he was no longer the British Middle East commander - the war in Europe took a startling new turn. With a mass of men and machines totaling 120 divisions, Adolf Hitler launched Operation Barbarossa, a surprise attack on Russia. To North Africa went Hitler's orders to "march in place" for the three or four months he predicted it would take to destroy the Russian Red Army.

Axis strategists foresaw glittering opportunities in Barbarossa. The conquest of southern Russia, they calculated, would become the upper jaw of an enormous pincers movement overwhelming the Middle East. Properly reinforced, Rommel would then sweep aside the British, thrust through Egypt, Palestine, Syria, and Iraq, force neutral Turkey to terms, and close the pincers in Persia. The Mediterranean would become an Axis lake; the Middle Eastern oil fields would fill the German war machine to capacity; the British would be severed from their empire and rendered helpless.

No one saw this promise more clearly than Erwin Rommel, although he knew for him the next few months would be crucial. He could expect no substantial reinforcements to be diverted from the Russian front. "It's all quiet here so far," he wrote his wife early in July. "But I'm not being taken in. Our stubborn friends on the other side will be back sooner or later."

Rommel's "stubborn friends" did indeed plan to test him again. Through the summer and fall of 1941, General Auchinleck rebuilt, reorganized, and even renamed his army. The desert force became the 8th Army, under the field command of General Sir Alan Cunningham. Planes, tanks, guns, trucks, and men by the thousands poured into Egypt from Great Britain; planes and tanks also came from American factories under the Lend-Lease program.

As British strength increased, Rommel's strength did not keep pace. Shortages of all kinds appeared as the Royal Air Force and Royal Navy slashed at his supply line across the Mediterranean. In

September 1941, 28 percent of all Axis cargoes were lost. In November, the figure leaped to 63 percent. In a night attack that month, a force of British warships pounced on a seven-ship convoy bound for Tripoli and sent all seven, plus an escorting Italian destroyer, to the bottom.

While the opponents gathered their forces, the siege of Tobruk dragged on, and skirmishes flickered around the outposts of the two armies. As patrols probed for information, the humped silhouettes of British armored cars and the squat, angular shapes of German cars became familiar sights on the horizon. Often they clashed, racing at each other in quick, darting sallies, blazing away with machine guns, skidding and swerving and throwing up plumes of dust. The loser might be left canted over in the sand under a spiral of oily black smoke, like some vanquished mechanical gladiator.

The search for accurate intelligence about enemy positions and movements never ceased. Armored-car patrols and aerial reconnaissance were effective ways to gain information quickly during battle. Another way was to send men deep behind enemy lines.

German units known as Brandenburgers penetrated into the rear of the 8th Army, sometimes nearly to Cairo, to gather information and attack supply lines. A more successful British unit called the Long Range Desert Group sent small parties of men in light trucks around the desert flank and well behind the enemy. Lurking near ports and along the coast road and the main desert tracks, they radioed information about the arrival of supply ships and kept track of the reinforcements sent to the Axis fighting forces. In November 1941, a group tried to kill or capture Rommel by raiding his headquarters,. but he was not there, and most of the raiders were killed or captured themselves.

Another British unit, the Special Air Service (a cover name to keep its real activities secret), not only gathered intelligence but spread havoc wherever it went. Set up in the summer of 1941 after Operation Battleaxe, the SAS' guiding genius was a handsome, six-foot-six, black-bearded young officer named David Stirling, the Phantom Major.

Ranging as far as 350 miles behind enemy lines and staying weeks at a time, SAS men menaced Rommel's supply lines and air support. They buried mines under the coast road, blew up gasoline stocks and supply dumps, attacked truck convoys, and shot up parked planes on airfields. In fourteen months of action, before Stirling was captured, the SAS destroyed 250 German and Italian aircraft.

A typical display of SAS daring was a raid that Stirling and two companions made on a German airfield near Benghazi. Approaching the field on a moonless night, they found two parked Messerschmitt 110 fighters. After attaching incendiary bombs with one-hour fuses to the planes, they turned to the hangars and workshops. They slipped into the first hangar, filled with machinery and tools, and planted more bombs. In the next hangar, four mechanics were repairing an engine. Keeping in the shadows, Stirling quietly placed a bomb in a Junkers transport plane only a few feet from the Germans. In the third hangar, the raiders found two more Junkers and stacks of crated aircraft engines, some forty in all. While one kept watch for patrolling guards, the other two planted bombs. It took them twenty minutes; now they were setting fuses for less than half an hour.

After coming within a hairbreadth of bumping into guards, Stirling decided to cap the night's work with a direct attack. As the time neared for the bombs to explode, he kicked open the door of the crowded guardroom and threw in a hand grenade. "We then ran like hell," one of his men wrote. "The bombs in the hangars had also started to go off. As we got clear, we stopped to look. One of the 110s on the field went up, and cannon started to explode with the heat. It was a pretty picture as the JU's in the hangars began to burn."

To spearhead the offensive, Operation Crusader, he had scheduled for November, General Cunningham put nearly all his armor - 4th, 7th, and 22nd armored brigades, averaging 155 cruiser tanks each - into the 30th Corps under General

Willoughby Norrie. He massed his infantry in another corps, the 13th, under General A.R. Godwin-Austen, and stiffened it with a brigade of 135 infantry tanks. Cunningham, whose brother commanded the Royal Navy in the Mediterranean, had made his mark beating the Italian army in East Africa, where he collected over 200,000 prisoners. This was to be his first chance to command a "tank army."

On the fighting line, the 8th Army could count some 600 tanks, with 100 more in besieged Tobruk and 200 in reserve. Cunningham intended to swing the armor of the 30th Corps around the desert flank of Rommel's frontier positions at Sallum and Bardia, drawing the German general into a tank battle. Once the panzer divisions were broken, the infantry of the 13th Corps would move in, mop up, and lift the siege of Tobruk. As to how the battle itself would be fought, Cunningham said, "My plans depend very much on what old Rommel decides to do."

Although the Axis forces received no significant reinforcements after Operation Battleaxe, some changes had been made. Rommel's major striking force remained the Afrika Korps, reorganized into three divisions - the 15th Panzer, the 21st Panzer (the old 5th Light Division renamed), and the 90th Light, an infantry division assembled from miscellaneous units - all under the command of

General Ludwig Cruwell. The bulk of Rommel's manpower was still Italian infantry.

The 8th Army had about 700 tanks to Rommel's 390. Nearly half of General Norrie's cruiser tanks were the new Crusaders, from which the assault took its name. They were fast and well armored, but weak mechanically. The Crusader, like the Matilda and its replacement, the Valentine, was armed with a two-pounder gun (named for the weight of its shell, forty-millimeter in diameter). From America had come the Stuart, mechanically sound, and at forty miles an hour, the fastest tank in the desert. Its high-velocity thirty-seven-millimeter gun hit slightly harder than the two-pounder, but its air-craft-type engine used so much gasoline that its combat range was short. The Stuart was popular with British tank crews, who christened it the Honey (a tanker described it as "a honey" after a test drive, and the name stuck).

On the Axis side, the work-horse tank was the Panzer Mark III, reliable, low to the ground, and mounting a short-barreled fifty-millimeter gun with about the same hitting power as the two-pounder; its armor was somewhat thin, however. Rommel also had thirty-five of the Panzer Mark IV. Its stubby seventy-five-millimeter gun was best suited to firing high-explosive shells at enemy infantry and artillery positions. His seventy Mark II light tanks mounted only heavy machine guns, and his 146 Italian tanks had poor armor and were liable to break down at any time.

The Afrika Korps did have an edge over the 8th Army in the quality of its antitank guns. The eighty-eight-millimeter was in a class by itself, although in the autumn of 1941, Rommel had only thirty-five of them. He had almost a hundred of the fifty-millimeter antitank guns, which outhit and outranged the two-pounder the British used as both a tank and antitank gun.

There were other, more fundamental differences in the two forces. In the German Army, a panzer division was a mixture of all arms - tanks, artillery, infantry, antitank guns - working in close cooperation. Rommel could shift his mobile forces anywhere on the battlefield without them being out of balance. This could not be done so easily in the 8th Army. Not only did the separate services - artillery, infantry, armor - jealously guard their independence, but Cunningham had a wide assortment of nationalities to deal with. Australians, Englishmen, Indians, New Zealanders, and South Africans had different military habits and did not always mesh when thrown together in an emergency.

The armies differed, too, in their handling of armor. The tank had been introduced in World War I by the British (with Winston Churchill as one of its chief developers). "Nothing so revolutionary in effect had occurred in warfare since the utilization of the horse, back in the mists of antiquity," wrote British military historian B.H. Liddell Hart. Britain lost her lead between the wars, however, and by World War II, lagged badly in tank tactics. Her generals tended to put armor into action piecemeal and to try to bull their way through defenses with tanks alone.

Rommel and other German armored commanders saw that tanks were most lethal against "thin-skinned" enemy forces - supply columns, infantry formations, artillery positions. The real counter to the tank was the antitank gun, and Rommel used these guns on offense as well as defense. If he could manage it, he would assault enemy armor with his antitank guns with his tanks in the line of advance; with the enemy tanks knocked out by these guns, his tanks would be free to flail at the unguarded enemy infantry and supply services.

Operation Crusader was to begin at dawn on November 18, 1941. Cunningham's forces moved into position the night before in a thunderstorm, the tanks and guns slithering through the mud, the infantry huddled together in their trucks against the cold, driving rain. All through the next day, the 8th Army, more than 100,000 strong, advanced across the empty desert under lowering storm clouds. There was no enemy to be seen. Committed to a battle plan based on what Rommel would do, Cunningham grew uneasy.

Rommel did not react because, for once, he had been surprised. British security and camouflage prevented German Intelligence from seeing the massing of the 8th Army. In addition, Rommel was preoccupied with an offensive against Tobruk that he had scheduled for November 21.

The 30th Corps initially moved around Rommel's flank with only two of its three armored brigades; the third was held back to help protect Godwin-Austen's infantry corps. Then, on November 19, the British armor became further divided. While the 7th Armored Brigade seized the Sidi Rezegh airfield, an important point that endangered Axis communications between Tobruk and the frontier, the 22nd Armored Brigade was to the south, skirmishing with the Italians, and the 4th Armored Brigade was to the east, embroiled in a sharp fight with a column from the Afrika Korps. Thoroughly alert now, Rommel prepared to throw his two panzer divisions into the battle.

November 20 was a day of march and countermarch and confusion as the generals tried to assess the situation. Groping for the enemy, Afrika Korps commander Cruwell ran one of his panzer divisions out of fuel. By late afternoon, however, he had tracked down General Alec Gatehouse's 4th Armored Brigade. For the second evening in a row, Gatehouse threw his American-built Honeys against the panzers and lost twenty-six of them. The 22nd Armored Brigade hurried from its forward position to help, but darkness put an end to the fighting.

On the fourth day of Crusader, the mood of the British high command ranged from elation to bewilderment. Early in the morning, Cruwell's panzers headed westward at high speed. As the 4th and 22nd armored brigades moved after them, Cairo headquarters flashed the news to the world that Rommel's army was in full retreat. The next day, American newspapers reported that half the German tanks were destroyed and that the panzer divisions were "pocketed" and their situation "appears desperate."

The British tankers of the 7th Armored Brigade had a different view of the matter. They were holding the Sidi Rezegh airfield, only ten miles from the Tobruk siege lines, which Rommel saw as key to the developing action. The Afrika Korps, far from retreating, was coming down hard on the 7th while holding off the two other slowly pursuing British armored brigades with a rear guard of antitank guns.

Attacking with antitank guns, the two panzer divisions began chewing up the 7th Armored Brigade. British infantry major Robin Hastings saw an enemy column approach the airfield over the

World War II: Desert War

rim of an escarpment. Five Crusader tanks rushing up to meet it were set aflame by antitank guns before their own two-pounders came within range. Three British antitank guns then took up the fight. "We watched these three guns firing away," recalled Major Hastings, "watched the crews, completely composed, completely undaunted, picked off one by one." When the Afrika Korps finally broke off, short of gasoline and ammunition, the gallant 7th Armored Brigade had only twenty-eight tanks left - but it still held the Sidi Rezegh airfield.

For the next forty-eight hours, Sidi Rezegh and the surrounding area was the scene of a savage, chaotic struggle. The airfield was strewn with disabled tanks and burned-out trucks, and the air was fogged with smoke and the dust churned up by thousands of vehicles. Supply columns snaked their way around the fringes of the ever-widening battle to feed fuel and ammunition to the fighters.

Neither high command was able to get a clear picture of what was going on. Often leadership came from lower-ranking officers who led from "up front." Captain Heinz Schmidt of a German rifle regiment wrote of directing a mixed panzer force against a South African position near the airfield on November 23. One after another the staff cars leading the charge were shot and their officers killed; finally, only Schmidt was left alive, lying wounded in a slit trench, despairing over the

58

failure of the advance. Then a young lieutenant came forward, rallied the leaderless force, and led it straight through the South Africans.

Before long, exhaustion and confusion began to exact their toll. When the Germans finally overran the Sidi Rezegh airfield, a British officer watched through binoculars as a column of dispirited, exhausted German infantrymen occupied the field, looking more like sleepwalkers than victors. Another officer confessed: "I can truthfully say that none of us had more than the vaguest idea where we were from day to day and hour to hour, or what was happening either to our own forces or the enemy's."

Robert Crisp of the 4th Armored Brigade told how the fight for the Sidi Rezegh airfield looked to a tank commander in the thick of it. "Twelve hundred yards ahead of me," Crisp wrote, "stretched the array of dark brown shapes, sixty or seventy monsters in a solid line abreast coming steadily towards the landing ground. The vicious flashes at the end of their gun muzzles stood out in fearful contrast against their camouflage. Behind them, the sky was blood-red.

"I picked up the mike to speak to the gunner: 'Cannon. Twelve hundred. . . . Pick out one and stay on it till you knock it out. Get cracking!' I heard the first shot go off almost immediately and watched the tracer sail in a long shallow curve. It hit on one of those dark silhouettes and bounded high into the air. We were much too far out of range to do any great damage, but I had to do something. . . .

"The air was full of lead and noise, and the tanks crept towards me with their guns belching. Mingled with the detonations of the high explosive shells and my own cannon I could hear that terrifying swish of armor-piercing shells and sometimes get a split-second glimpse of a tracer going by, taking the breath out of my lungs with the vacuum of its passage. Every now and again my Honey would give that quick lurch, which meant a hit.

"I heard my gunner yell 'I've got one, sir!' and it sounded good to hear his elation and to see the slow smoke curling up from the Mark III and the men bail out. The gunner was all right. . . . The loader was all right too. He would be too busy to be scared - tugging the next shell out of its bracket, pulling down the ejection lever, whipping in a new shell with enough force to close the breech, bending under to tap the gunner in the 'gun ready' signal, and then starting all over again. . . .The driver was the chap I felt sorry for. He would be squeezed back and to one side, getting as far away from his driving slit [in the armor] as possible, inactive and frightened to death. . . .

"I had a last despairing search behind me for some sign of rescue and support, and then I decided to go. . . . I said as quietly as I could into the mike:

'Gunner, cease fire. Driver, advance - turn about - go like hell!'

"That 'driver, advance' was the critical moment. It was always the same after a slugging match with the enemy; that frantic second of time when you did not know whether the tank would move or not. Even if the engine is still running, the suspension may be blasted; either of the tracks may be lying on the sand in mangled pieces; any of those sickening lurches might have meant the end of your last hope - mobility. I held my breath and felt the tank heave as the gears engaged. Then the engine seemed to rev high with relief, and the tank moved forward. . . .

"We got round the turn-about without disaster, and soon we were speeding back across the airfield, jinking left and right, creating our own smoke screen of dust. . . . So we fled back, running that incredible gauntlet of death, each second beckoning us to safety. . . ."

The testing of men in war is cruel and searching - and one quality that separates the great general from the merely good one - is a relentless probing for an opposing commander's weakness. On the night of November 23, General Cunningham at 8th Army headquarters believed he had lost the tank battle upon which Operation Crusader hinged. Some 300 of his cruisers had been knocked out; as far as he could see, withdrawal to protect his "thin-skinned" infantry was his only choice.

Rommel had measured Cunningham by the way he conducted his battle and found him wanting. "What difference does it make if you have two tanks to my one," Rommel was to tell a captured British officer after the battle, "when you spread them out and let me smash them in detail? You presented me with three brigades in succession!" With a sixth sense for reading his opponent's mind, he conceived a stroke that violated military logic, but was well calculated to press Cunningham into retreat. At mid-morning on November 24, with all his armor (the Afrika Korps had only ninety tanks remaining), Rommel left the battlefield entirely and raced eastward to the Egyptian border, seeking to wreck the 8th Army's communications and supply lines and overrun its infantry.

What Rommel did not know, however, was that the man he was aiming at no longer held the power of decision. Matters were now in the hands of General Auchinleck. The commander had flown from Cairo to 8th Army headquarters the night before to be briefed on the crisis and to hear Cunningham's recommendations. Claude Auchinleck was a big, powerful, decisive man with strong opinions and a stubborn streak. He realized that Rommel, too, had suffered heavily; outnumbered from the start, the Germans could ill afford their losses. He refused to withdraw. The next morning, as the Afrika Korps was setting off for the frontier, he sent a curt directive to Cunningham: "You will . . . continue to attack the enemy relentlessly, using all your resources even to the last tank."

Auchinleck's decision - certainly as bold as Rommel's raid – would eventually turn the tide of battle. The German panzers were successful in "clipping the tail" of the 8th Army, and they came very close to stumbling on the two huge supply dumps upon which the whole army depended. War correspondent Alan Moorehead, who was with the supply units caught up in the raid, called it a stampede. "All day for nine hours we ran," he wrote. "It was the contagion of bewilderment and fear and ignorance." But because of Auchinleck's firmness, the British fighting forces were hardly affected. After indecisively milling about in the frontier area, the Afrika Korps returned to aid its beleaguered infantry comrades at Sidi Rezegh.

The Crusader battle dragged on for ten more days. General Cunningham was replaced as head of the 8th Army by General Neil Ritchie. By then, the British brigade commanders ran the battle. Sidi Rezegh changed hands three times; however, superior strength and reserves began to tell. The 8th Army and the Tobruk garrison linked up, and by December 7, Rommel was down to thirty tanks. He had to give up the battlefield, give up the siege of Tobruk, and retreat. (That same day, halfway around the world, Japan attacked Pearl Harbor; now Britain and America were full war partners.)

With the advancing British, correspondent Moorehead examined the Sidi Rezegh airfield, where so much of the Crusader fighting had taken place. Everywhere he saw graves - marked with a helmet or a belt, some with simple crosses made from packing cases and bearing penciled names. "Sometimes there were mingled German and British graves," he wrote, "as though the men had gone down together, still locked in fighting. Sometimes the dead were laid alongside the blackened hulks of their burnt-out tanks. . . . You could see the mess boxes, the toothbrushes, and blankets of the crews scattered around together with their little packets of biscuits, their water bottles, photographs of their families. . . . Like great lizards, the broken tracks of tanks were sprawled across the sand with their teeth gaping upward. . . . Over everything hung the bleak winter's sky."

Rommel continued to withdraw through Cyrenaica, steadily but without panic. On Christmas Eve, the pursuing British occupied Benghazi. By early January 1942, Rommel was at El Agheila, back where he had started nine months before. The Axis frontier positions at Bardia and Sallum, now entirely cut off, had to surrender.

Crusader was unquestionably a British victory,

for it achieved its goals - the relief of Tobruk, the destruction of the bulk of the German armor, and the recapture of Cyrenaica. Still, there was little of the pride and elation that had greeted the Wavell-O'Connor victory over the Italians the winter before. Too many mistakes had been made, too much strength had been frittered away, too many men and machines had been lost needlessly. Rommel, the Desert Fox, had somehow managed to dominate the battle even in defeat.

Rommel, in fact, refused to stay beaten. On January 17, 1942, he wrote his wife: "I'm full of plans that I daren't say anything about around here [to the Italian high command]. They'd think me crazy. But I'm not; I simply see a bit farther than they do. . . ." Four days later, his tank strength reinforced to about 100, the Desert Fox launched a counterstrike that took the British - and the German and Italian high commands as well - by surprise.

Driving his men hard, rapidly shifting the weight of his attack from one column to another, Rommel scattered the British formations in Cyrenaica. He feinted his enemy out of Benghazi, capturing huge stocks of supplies and fuel to keep his offensive moving. In two whirlwind weeks, the 8th Army was again driven out of the Cyrenaican bulge and into a defensive position at Gazala, thirty-five miles west of Tobruk.

This counterstroke, beyond recapturing the port of Benghazi and critical Cyrenaican airfields, was more than anything else a moral victory. It enlarged the Desert Fox's reputation for invincibility; he might be checked, but he had yet to be defeated. It remained to be seen how much this reputation would weigh on the scales of future battles.

Incident at Sidi Rezegh

The speed and confusion of armored warfare can be glimpsed in this account by Robert Crisp, a South African who before the war had been an internationally known cricket star. It is from his book *Brazen Chariots*. On November 27, 1941, the tenth day of the Crusader battle, Crisp's squadron of Honey tanks surprised a convoy of German supply trucks on a desert track called the Trigh Capuzzo, near Sidi Rezegh.

> The Honeys positively leaped over the top of the ridge and plunged down the steady incline to the Trigh. We were half-way down the slope and going like bats out of hell in the bright sunlight before the Jerries realized what was happening. Then the familiar pattern of alarm and confusion and panic-flight away from us at right angles to the road. . . .
>
> Within seconds, the dust was full of the crisscross pattern of tracers drawing

red lines through the yellow cloud and puncturing the fleeing dark shapes with deadly points. From the turret tops we let go with tommy-guns and revolvers, and every now and again the whip-crack of the 37mm interjected the staccato chatter of the Browning [machine gun]. I could still see a Honey or two racing alongside, but what was happening beyond the narrow limits of vision I could only guess.

Suddenly, through the dust, I saw the flat plane of the ground disappear into space. I yelled like mad at the driver to halt. He had seen the danger only a fraction of a second after I had, and jerked back on the brakes even while I was shouting at him. The tracks locked fast and we skidded to a violent stop with the front sprockets hanging over a sharp drop that started the descent of a steep escarpment. . . .

I became aware of an astonishing scene at the foot of the escarpment, where it leveled out into a broad wadi. Vehicles of all shapes and sizes were everywhere - some upright and still moving away as fast as they could; others stationary and bewildered; many lying on their sides or backs with the wheels poking grotesquely upwards. Dark figures of men darted wildly about.

Even as I watched, a great lorry went plunging down the escarpment out of control; it struck some outcrop and leaped high into the air somersaulting to the bottom in a fantastic avalanche of earth, rock, and scrub and odd-shaped bundles of men interspersed with jagged pieces of wood and metal. The concentration of transport in the wadi below was a wonderful target. I said quickly into the mouthpiece: "Both guns. Fire with everything you've got. . . ."

Suddenly there was a fearful bang, and simultaneously I was drenched from head to foot with an astonishing cascade of cold water. For a moment or two, I was physically and mentally paralyzed. I just could not believe that anything like that could happen. Then realization came swiftly and terribly - the water tins on the back of the tank had been hit. It could mean only one thing. As I looked backwards I was already giving the order to the gunner to traverse the turret as fast as he bloody well could.

In one flash I saw it all, and the fear leaped in me. Not fifty yards away a fifty-millimeter antitank gun pointed straight at the Honey, pointed straight between my eyes. Beyond it were other guns and the sight I had dreaded most - a number of motionless Honeys and the huddled figures of our black-bereted men crouched on the sand or stretched out in the agony of death.

It took less than a second for the whole scene and its awful meaning to register in my mind. I could see the German gunners slamming the next shell into the breech as the turret whirled. I yelled, "Machine gun, fire!" In the same moment, I saw the puff of smoke from the antitank gun and felt and heard the strike on the armor plating. Quickly I looked down into the turret. A foot or two below me the gunner was staring at his hand, over which a dark red stain was slowly spreading. Then he gave a scream and fell groveling on the floor. In the top right hand corner of the turret, a jagged hole gaped, and through it, like some macabre peepshow, I could see the gun being reloaded. . . .

I leaned down and pulled the trigger of the Browning, and kept my finger there until the gun jammed. God knows where the bullets went. Twice I felt the Honey shudder and the second time more water came pouring in. When the Browning stopped and my mind leaped about searching for some way to stay alive I suddenly saw the slim chance. If the tank would move at all, we could drop over the edge of the escarpment, we would be out of sight of those blasted antitank guns. I said urgently into the mike: "Driver, advance. Over the edge. Quick!"

I felt the gears engage, and for a split second the world stood still. Then the engine revved, and the Honey heaved forward and dropped with a violent crash over the escarpment. In the turret, we were hurled about like corks, and then the bouncing stopped and we rode smoothly down the slope. . . .

So much had happened in a few minutes, or a few hours it might have been, and I had looked so closely into the valley of the shadow, that I found it difficult to return to reality. I just could not fully absorb our situation. . . . We were chugging along casually through the deserted silence of the wadi. It was uncanny after the tumult and terror just behind us. . . .

The unreality persisted when the Honey swung right in response to my order, and moved slowly up the slope to the crest. As soon as my eyes were above the lip of the escarpment we halted, and the full picture of horror burst on me immediately.

Not much more than 500 yards away, like a projection on a cinema screen, lay the battlefield. My eyes lifted to the tall black columns, leaning slightly with the wind, and followed them down to the Honeys gasping smoke. Four of my tanks were blazing infernos; three others just sat there, sad and abandoned. A line of antitank guns with their crews still manning them expectantly, lined the edge of the drop. The whole scene was silhouetted sharply against the yellow clouds of dust which rose in a thick fog from the wadi below. I could see many men running about between guns and tanks and vehicles. My heart ached as I picked out the familiar bereted figures of our own troops, huddled in disconsolate groups or being shepherded singly by gesturing Germans. . . .

CHAPTER 4
DESERT CRISIS

For some three and a half months, early in 1942, an uneasy lull settled over the Western Desert. The two armies lay inert at Gazala, exhausted by their heavy losses in the winter battles, while in Berlin, Cairo, London, and Rome their masters debated grand strategy.

The German blitzkrieg in Russia had bogged down as it met stiffening resistance and the frigid winter, and heavy arms shipments from Britain and the United States were helping to keep the Red Army alive. As he hatched plans for a renewed assault on Russia, Hitler looked once more at that grand scheme for a Middle Eastern pincers movement suggested a year before. Now he envisioned the lower jaw of such a pincers thrusting against

Russia's vulnerable southern flank, perhaps even linking up with the Japanese advancing from the Far East. But standing in the way were the British 8th Army at Gazala and the island of Malta in the Mediterranean.

Behind the desert battles raged the grim, unseen, unceasing battle of supply. The British supply line around Africa was 14,000 miles and six weeks long, yet it was relatively safe from attack. Rommel's lifeline stretched only from Italy and Sicily across the Mediterranean to Tripoli, but it was vulnerable to air and sea attack every mile of the way. Malta was the key. The small British island sixty miles south of Sicily armed the planes and submarines that harassed the Axis supply routes. The Royal Navy's only other bases were at Alexandria and Gibraltar, at opposite ends of the Mediterranean; the only other RAF fields were in Cyrenaica (when the British held that area, which in early 1942 they did not) and Egypt.

In April and May of 1942, the Luftwaffe set about removing Malta from Britain's Mediterranean chessboard. Wave after wave of bombers and fighters pounded the island. Air-raid sirens wailed all hours of the day and night; in April, the alerts averaged nine a day. Dockyards, supply depots, and airfields suffered heavily, and food stocks dipped perilously low. Twice the American aircraft carrier *Wasp* slipped secretly into the Mediterranean, made a high-speed dash eastward, and launched RAF Spitfires to bolster the island's fighter defenses.

Malta survived on a diet of stubborn courage, but its sting was gone. Axis convoys steamed across the Mediterranean to unload gasoline and tanks and guns for Rommel. For the only time in his North African campaigns, the Desert Fox got nearly the supplies he needed.

The Germans had plans to seize Malta, as they had the island of Crete the year before. But with the Luftwaffe's success, it was decided to let Rommel strike the first blow. He would open his Western Desert offensive in late May. If and when he reached the Egyptian frontier, he was to pause while Malta was taken. With that thorn removed from his side, the great campaign could resume.

As Malta's agony continued, Churchill's short temper grew shorter. In Russia, the German steamroller was gathering speed again. In the Pacific and the Far East, the Japanese advanced unchecked. At home, Britons grumbled about the way the government was running the war. Since only in North Africa were the British at grips with the German Army, Churchill stepped up the pressure on Auchinleck to attack, win a desert victory, and restore Britain's morale and prestige. On May 10, the pressure was put as a direct order. Plans for an early offensive, code-named Operation Buckshot, were prepared.

As strategy was hammered out in the war councils, troops in the Western Desert sat and waited. The heat and the dust and the crawling flies did not make the waiting comfortable. Raw "desert sores," intestinal diseases, and plagues of sand fleas added to the torment. Off duty there was nothing to do and nowhere to go, except perhaps to the Mediterranean once a week for a swim.

The only thing more monotonous than the routine and the terrain was the army food. The 8th Army staple was canned corned beef, or bully, that had all the flavor of sawdust. In Rommel's army, the counterpart of bully was an Italian sausage labeled A.M., A.M.'s with such tough stringiness that soon had the Germans were calling it *Alter Mann*, or "old man." Italian soldiers were more candid - they called it *Asino Morte*, "dead donkey." Whenever either side seized the other's rations, of course, bully or A.M. quickly became a delicacy.

No two armies ever hammered each other more savagely in battle, but they gradually developed a bond as close to a code of chivalry as the war produced. Perhaps the reason was their mutual dislike of the barren land they struggled for; perhaps it was the absence of secret police and concentration camps and conquered populations; or perhaps it was simply the decency of the generals who led both armies. Whatever the reasons, the war in North Africa saw few of the atrocities that stained other battlefields of World War II. Prisoners were not mistreated. Flags of truce were honored to remove dead and wounded after a battle, and doctors treated friend and foe impartially.

This bond also grew out of a shared stock of desert legends. Men on both sides chuckled over the time that the Long Range Desert Group popped up miles from nowhere and made off with the drowsy Italian garrison of an oasis fort without a shot being fired, or the exploit of the German scout who appropriated a British military policeman's cap and directed an entire 8th Army supply convoy up a side track and "into the bag." They recounted the tale of the British division commander who, within forty-eight hours, was nabbed twice and twice escaped and then spent an entire day hiding in a dry cistern while a tank battle raged around him, or of Rommel suddenly appearing at a British field hospital at the height of the Crusader fight, inquiring about the welfare of the wounded and the stock of medicines, then driving off again before the startled staff realized how easily they could have captured him. And every night at ten o'clock, radios all over the desert were turned on, and Allied and Axis soldiers alike sat quietly and stared across the dark landscape and thought of home as they listened to a European short-wave station serenade them with a sad and sentimental German ballad called "Lili Marlene."

As the weeks dragged by, the two armies slowly rebuilt their strength. General Ritchie's 8th Army welcomed shipments of new tanks and new antitank guns. From America came the Grant, a big, awkward-looking tank that packed a hefty wallop. In addition to a thirty-seven-millimeter gun in a revolving turret, the Grant had a powerful seventy-five-millimeter gun mounted in the hull. This gun had a limited field of fire - it was aimed by aiming the tank itself - yet it outranged and outhit any other tank gun on the British side. The new antitank gun was the six-pounder, a fifty-seven-millimeter weapon with good range and penetrating power. By May, the 8th Army had over a hundred six-pounders, although their crews lacked the proper armor-piercing ammunition for them.

As for Rommel's corps, its heavy tank losses in Crusader were made good during Malta's pounding. Rommel had 223 Panzer Mark III's with the fifty-millimeter gun but with considerably thicker armor. He also had nineteen of the new Mark III Specials, each mounting a long-barreled, high-velocity fifty-millimeter gun with half again the hitting power of the short gun of the same caliber. The tanks of the Italian Ariete armored division were little improved from the days of Marshal Graziani, and their embittered crews called them "self-propelled coffins." Rommel had a total of 560 tanks to Ritchie's 843 (including 167

American Grants), but his antitank-gun strength was superior. The two air forces were about equal.

Ritchie could not get Operation Buckshot ready before June 1942. Meanwhile, the 8th Army stretched across forty miles of desert south of Gazala, arranged in heavily fortified "boxes" strung together by mine fields. The armored brigades were positioned behind this line. At nine o'clock on the evening of May 26, the detailed plans for Buckshot went into the trash as Rommel struck first.

Under a bright moon, column after column of trucks and guns and tanks rolled forward. The Afrika Korps, some 10,000 vehicles strong, curled around Bir Hacheim, the southern anchor of Ritchie's Gazala Line. A British officer on patrol reported to headquarters: "Looks like a brigade of Jerry tanks coming." Then he looked again at the size of the dust cloud: "It's more than a brigade - it's the whole bloody Afrika Korps!"

For some reason, 8th Army headquarters was slow in getting and analyzing such reports. In the early hours of May 27, Rommel pushed northward behind the Gazala Line, surprising some British units eating breakfast. Two motorized infantry brigades and the headquarters of an armored formation was overrun. Despite these first successes, the Afrika Korps was in deep trouble by afternoon. The British put in uncoordinated but hard counterattacks and knocked out a third of

Rommel's tanks; the long-range guns of the Grants came as a particular shock to the Germans.

May 28 was a day of confusion, with armored clashes flaring up at every point of the compass and a massive sandstorm blanketing the battlefield. The Axis supply situation grew critical as truck convoys floundered on the long route around Bir Hacheim. As usual, Rommel was leading from up front, narrowly escaping injury in brushes with British columns and once being shelled by Italian artillery. That night he personally led supply convoys to the stranded panzer divisions.

As the Battle of Gazala raged through its third day, and the British command continued to act sluggishly, Rommel decided to go on the defensive temporarily to bind up his army's wounds. Instead of retreating, he lodged himself in a nest of British minefields in the center of the Gazala Line. Sappers (mine-removal crews) cut corridors through the mine fields at his back to open a direct route to his supply dumps and to the Italian infantry divisions facing the British in the north. Rommel's bridgehead came to be known as the Cauldron.

With this unexpected stroke, the Desert Fox once more confounded his opponent. General Ritchie could find no easy way to cope with the Cauldron. A frontal attack on the massed Afrika Korps was not an appealing prospect. If he reached out beyond the Gazala Line to threaten Rommel's supply line, he would expose his own supply dumps to an armored strike from the Cauldron. Unable to decide what to do, Ritchie and his generals fell to bickering.

Rommel set about consolidating his new position. In the center of it was the troublesome British 150th Brigade box, steadily shelling his supply corridors through the mine fields. While the screen of antitank guns held off the British armor, Rommel threw his full weight at the 150th Brigade. It fought for more than two days, to the last round of ammunition, before it was overwhelmed.

By June 5, the tenth day of the battle, General Ritchie had evolved a plan: a frontal attack on the Cauldron. "If ever an operation resembled sticking one's arm into a wasp's nest, this did," concluded one historian. On paper the plan, codenamed Aberdeen, was complicated but promising; in practice, it was a disaster. Units advanced in the wrong place at the wrong time; infantry attacked unsupported by armor; armor was not backed by artillery. The two armored brigades involved lost 118 tanks, half their strength, and in the confusion, an Indian infantry brigade was left stranded within the Cauldron. After driving the British armor away, Rommel attacked the Indians the next day, all but wiping them out.

A British gunner recorded the death agonies of Aberdeen. "The next attack came in very quickly," he wrote, "and soon German tanks had overrun the infantry battalion in the rear and were nosing about the burning vehicles. . . . Events moved quickly now, and amazing things happened as the fighting raged at close quarters. A sergeant of the reconnaissance regiment with what was left of his section leaped on a German tank, trying to ram hand grenades through the turret. They were killed to a man. The machine-gun fire was intense. . . .

"The doctor and his orderly worked unceasingly in a murderous fire round the Command Post, which was a shambles of dead and wounded. . . . Of the antitank guns only one now remained, but there was no one to man it until a young lance-bombardier, with one arm blown off at the elbow, crawled out in a vain attempt to reach it. . . .

"The end was very near now. . . . The survivors of the battery turned sadly to their final task - the battering of their gun sights. For a few moments more, the air sang with machine-gun bullets; then all was quiet, and that deep silence that descends on a battlefield when the contest is over spread over the Cauldron. . . ."

After his rout of Operation Aberdeen, Rommel turned his attention to the French garrison defending Bir Hacheim at the southern end of the Gazala Line. "Seldom in Africa was I given such a hard-fought struggle," he admitted. He led several assaults himself, and Luftwaffe Stukas dropped bomb after bomb into the defenses. Finally, the Frenchmen could hold out no longer, and on the night of June 10, the survivors broke out. All the while, the rest of the 8th Army had "kept astonishingly quiet" (in Rommel's words), its high command seemingly paralyzed by the pace of events.

With his supply line secure and the southern half of the Gazala Line in his hands, the Desert Fox was ready to resume the offensive. The British line was now bent back at a right angle, with its hinge in an area known as Knightsbridge. On June 11, the Afrika Korps sprang out of the Cauldron toward Knightsbridge and mauled the confused and disorganized British armored brigades one after another. The desert was strewn with derelict Crusaders and Grants and Stuarts, some of them only slightly damaged or out of fuel. But the British left the field, and with them went any hope of recovering and repairing these casualties. On June 11, Ritchie reported a tank force of 330; on the fourteenth he had seventy. Knightsbridge became the blackest name in the 8th Army's history.

There was nothing for Ritchie to do now but pick up the pieces and retreat. The only escape corridor left open for the British infantry was the coast road passing through Tobruk. The Luftwaffe pitched into the columns of trucks and guns crawling eastward, and the "Gazala Gallop" began.

"Stragglers from other units cut in among the battalion transport and force the pace," begins a South African's account. "As the battalion vehicles try to regain their place, convoy discipline begins to go: a panicking few are breaking up the disciplined many. . . . The road is relentlessly machine-gunned and bombed. Trucks blaze. Men run; ambulances howl towards the hospital in Tobruk; dead men lie in blood and oil and broken glass. . . ."

By June 15, the 8th Army was a beaten army, and Neil Ritchie was a beaten general. Rommel not only had a firm grip on the initiative, but for the first time, he had a substantial edge in tanks. That night he wrote his wife jubilantly. "The enemy is breaking up. . . . We've made a pretty clear sweep this time." The next stop, he vowed, was Tobruk.

To Rommel and Churchill, the two men who would decide its fate, Tobruk was more than anything else a symbol. No matter that it was now militarily indefensible, its minefields incomplete, its antitank ditches so full of drifted sand that they "would hardly have interfered with the progress of a garden roller." No matter that its harbor facilities couldn't handle the supply needs of Afrika Korps on a drive to the Suez Canal. Rommel would not rest until he had conquered the fortress that had defeated him; the prime minister would not hear of its being abandoned. "Presume there is no question in any case of giving up Tobruk," he imperiously signaled Auchinleck on June 14.

Even as Auchinleck and Ritchie cobbled together a force to defend Tobruk, Rommel cut off the fortress and issued orders for an attack. Promptly at first light on June 20, more than 200 German and Italian aircraft unleashed a torrent of bombs on the defenses, and the massed artillery of the Afrika Korps added to the destruction. Moving behind the curtain of shells, German shock troops and engineers cracked the outer defense line, capturing many stunned defenders in their underground bunkers. Then the tanks moved forward through the gap, Rommel leading the way.

By early afternoon, the 15th and 21st panzer divisions were enveloping Tobruk's strong points one by one. At the vital King's Cross road-junction, Rommel stood on the roof of his armored command car watching the progress of the battle through binoculars as bewildered British prisoners streamed by him. By evening, the 21st Panzer was in the streets of Tobruk itself. Just then a relief column sent out by Ritchie was at Sidi Rezegh. "In the distance to the north," wrote one of its officers, "straight in the direction of the fortress, a great black cloud began to rise. Many of us had seen that cloud before, the token over a year before of the impending surrender of the Italians. Now we knew that the dumps, the great oil tanks, the supplies accumulated for our offensive to Benghazi, had been set on fire. . . ."

Through a night lit by flares and noisy with the stutter of machine guns and the harsh grinding of tanks, Tobruk's commander, South African general H.B. Klopper, tried to organize a breakout. But there was too little time and too few trucks. "Situation shambles," he signaled Ritchie. "Terrible casualties would result," he said, if he continued the fight. Shortly after dawn on June 21, a white flag was raised over Klopper's headquarters.

More than 32,000 prisoners and some 2,000 vehicles fell into Axis hands; more important, 2,000 tons of precious gasoline were seized before the defenders could destroy it. German troops rooted happily through the captured stores, filling up on South African pineapple, Irish potatoes, English beer - just as the Australians had reveled among the Italian stores captured in Tobruk in January 1941. Rommel did not pause to gloat. "Fortress of Tobruk has capitulated," he announced to his army. "All units will reassemble and prepare for further advance." Hitler immediately promoted him to the rank of field marshal.

The news was a great tonic to the German public. In Berlin, a neutral Swedish newspaperman watched celebrating crowds and reported that he had not seen such gaiety there since the fall of France in 1940. Winston Churchill was in the United States, meeting with President Roosevelt. He had just finished breakfast and had joined Roosevelt in the

White House study. Without a word, the president handed him a message telling of Tobruk's surrender. "This was one of the heaviest blows I can recall during the war," Churchill was to write later. "I did not attempt to hide from the president the shock I had received. It was a bitter moment. Defeat is one thing; disgrace is another. . . ."

As Rommel drove his army eastward once more, officers from the German and Italian high commands reminded him that he was to halt until Malta was taken - Luftwaffe support would be needed for the attack on the island. The Desert Fox stormed at them that the 8th Army was vulnerable, and it might never be again. When Marshal Ettore Bastico, commander of all Axis forces in North Africa, issued a direct order to stop, Rommel replied that he would "not accept the advice" and invited Bastico to dine with him in Cairo. Finally, Hitler had to intervene, remarking that "it is only once in a lifetime that the Goddess of Victory smiles." The pursuit would go on. Malta would not be assaulted.

"How can one describe the retreat of a modern army?" wrote British correspondent Denis Johnston. "The roaring, rattling caterpillar of battered trucks and dirty men - the great transporters shouldering broken-down tanks, the RAF recovery lorries towing wrecked aircraft, the field kitchens and the ambulances . . . this mass of machinery churning the dust and spewing out petrol fumes, entangled in traffic blocks and then grinding onwards again. . . . Tractors and bulldozers - staff cars and clattering machine-gun carriers - armored control vehicles and map lorries - trucks breaking off from the column and bumping violently across the margins of sand and scrub, followed by long trails of brown dust - trucks lining up for petrol - trucks in their tens and in their hundreds and in their thousands clanging and roaring their way eastward. . . ."

On June 23, two days after Tobruk's fall, Rommel's forces reached the Egyptian frontier. The two German armored divisions had forty-four tanks between them, the Italians fourteen more. Infantry units were at skeleton strength, totaling about 2,500 German and 6,000 Italian. Four out of every five trucks were British, running on captured fuel. But Rommel's domination of his enemy was virtually complete. Ritchie could think of nothing but "to gain time with distance." His goal was a defensive position at Matruh, 120 miles inside the frontier. He arrived there on June 25, with Rommel on his heels.

As Ritchie got his forces ready for battle, he announced that the retreat was over, that the 8th Army would make its fight at Matruh and die there if it lost. That evening, General Auchinleck, as he had done in the Crusader battle seven months before, flew up from Cairo and took command of the army. Matruh was not where the 8th Army would win or die, he decided. It must remain "in being" no matter how far it had to retreat if there was any hope of saving the Middle East.

Auchinleck had no time to make his presence felt before Rommel attacked. The Battle of Matruh was surely the most astonishing of the Desert Fox's career. Late on June 26, he drove what was left of the Afrika Korps through a nine-mile gap between the halves of the 8th Army. The next day, he resumed the advance, leaving the 90th Light Division, reduced to 1,600 men, to mask the entire British 10th Corps in Matruh. The panzer divisions tangled with some 150 British tanks assembled to the south.

The fighting was inconclusive, and the Afrika Korps was in a perilous position by dusk. The 90th Light lay isolated on the coast road east of Matruh, "cutting off" five whole brigades of British infantry. The 21st Panzer Division, with fourteen tanks and 600 infantrymen, "surrounded" a fresh New Zealand division just brought up from the Nile delta. The 15th Panzer Division, twenty tanks strong, was to the west, facing two brigades of British armor.

British Intelligence, however, credited Rommel with four times as many German tanks as he had; in addition, the Rommel legend was now in full bloom. British General "Strafer" Gott, who had been fighting in the desert since O'Connor's offensive in 1940, was under the spell of the legend that day. Believing the battle had been lost, he ordered the armor to withdraw. The 8th Army's position collapsed. The New Zealanders, unsupported by any armor after Gott's withdrawal, broke through the encircling 21st Panzer that night in a wild melee. On the next night, the 10th Corps in Matruh pushed aside the 90th Light and also broke out. The Afrika Korps collected some 6,000 prisoners, more than its own total manpower. The Gazala Gallop continued, the next stop El Alamein, sixty miles from Alexandria.

As June turned to July, it seemed that the end was near for the Allies in the Middle East. On June 29, Benito Mussolini flew to Cyrenaica to prepare for the victory parade he would lead through the streets of Cairo; he took with him a white charger to provide the proper Caesar-like image. Panic played over Alexandria and Cairo like summer lightning. The Royal Navy hastily pulled out of its base at Alexandria and steamed through the Suez Canal to the safety of the Red Sea. Great clouds of smoke rose over military headquarters in Cairo as clerks (the Short Range Desert Group, combat soldiers called them) burned bales of secret documents. So great was the fall of charred paper from their bonfires that July 1, 1942, became famous as "Ash Wednesday."

Beneath these ripples of panic, however, the 8th Army was getting a grip on itself. There are no soldiers more stubborn than British soldiers, and they gradually came to see what Rommel had gotten away with at Matruh. Auchinleck stood by the coast road, watching the trucks and guns and tanks roll into the El Alamein position, and he thought that the men were tired and angry but that their morale was good; what they needed most was leadership. On June 30, he issued an order to his troops: "The enemy is stretching to his limit and thinks we are a broken army. . . . He hopes to take Egypt by bluff. Show him where he gets off." It was an entirely accurate reading of the situation.

The Afrika Korps was at the end of its tether. Its main supply line stretched almost 1,400 miles to Tripoli. Malta was back in business smashing Axis convoys. In an around-the-clock effort, the RAF was decimating its columns with bombs and bullets. And its men were dead on their feet. "Rommel has wonderful energy himself," a German prisoner said, "but he drives us too hard, and some of us can't take much more of this."

Through July, the two armies slugged groggily at each other at El Alamein. Rommel and Auchinleck were no longer able to inspire their exhausted officers and men to that extra effort needed for victory; the two commanders, said an observer, "were full of fire, but could not keep the battle aflame." On both sides, opportunities were missed, mistakes were made. In one attack, an armored brigade fresh from England was hit hard by antitank fire, blundered into an uncharted minefield, and lost almost all its 104 tanks. The Italian Ariete Division let itself be surprised by the New Zealanders and lost nearly all its artillery. "Things are going downright badly for me at the moment," Rommel wrote his wife on July 17. "The enemy is using his superiority, especially in infantry, to destroy the Italian formations one by one, and the German formations are much too weak to stand alone. It's enough to make one weep."

The crisis was over, the high-tide mark reached. Rommel's brilliant campaign was history; at El Alamein in July 1942, he lost the initiative. By personal strength and unswerving purpose, Claude Auchinleck had ended the Gazala Gallop. Rommel himself delivered the final verdict: "Although the British losses . . . had been higher than ours, yet the price to Auchinleck had not been excessive, for the thing that had mattered to him was to halt our advance, and that, unfortunately, he had done."

Incident at Matruh

The Battle of Matruh, the climax of Rommel's 1942 campaign, was decided when the British armor withdrew. On the night of June 27-28, the 2nd New Zealand Division was ordered to break through the thin ring placed around it by the 21st Panzer Division. These excerpts describe the breakout.

The fast first and third are from *Infantry Brigadier*, a book by New Zealand's General Howard Kippenberger; the second account is by Lieutenant Colonel G. P. Hanna, taken from the history of the Royal Artillery.

> I was called to Division for a conference about eight o'clock that evening [June 27]., We stood in a group at the back of the command truck. Brigadier Inglis said that all attacks had been repulsed so far, but the enemy was fairly round behind us and we obviously were in a grave position. The going to the south was reported bad, the only sure going was due east, which meant that we must make a breakthrough. . . .
>
> The trucks were packed to the limit and the hundreds of men whom they could not carry were crammed on to the fighting vehicles. Men were hanging on wherever there was standing room, squeezed inside the gun quads, on the guns themselves, on carriers and antitank gun haulers, everywhere imaginable. The loading was completed in a quiet and orderly manner and I walked round to check up. I found about twenty men still unaccommodated and they followed me round while I found places for them one by one. . . .
>
> At last, well after midnight [writes Colonel

Hanna], we started to move forward, the column led by the Royal Artillery brigadier. The 4th Brigade had not completed its attack, but we were forced to begin the breakout so that we should have a long enough period of darkness in which to get well clear of the enemy. We passed slowly through 4th Brigade's old area. There was little small-arms fire ahead of us, and later we learned that 4th Brigade had done tremendous execution with the bayonet.

We had gone only a short distance past the original forward posts when the scouting carriers moving just ahead of the column halted. A moment later the darkness in front exploded into fire. Tank shells and machine-gun bullets poured into the column, and a number of our vehicles burst into flames, illuminating the whole area.

We remained halted in reality for only a few seconds, uncertain what to do. Then the brigadier roared out from his jeep, "Follow me!" Several of us in the leading vehicles did so, and we drove hard right, that is, south, skirting the enemy tanks. The whole column followed. The going was poor, but any thought of cautious driving was abandoned. We had gone about 500 yards when more enemy tanks immediately in front of us opened fire. We halted again, and our predicament was obviously much more serious this time. Many of the leading vehicles went up in flames, a single shell in some cases going through two or three trucks in line.

My recollections are a little vague at this point, but I remember that, with no alternative, we started up and drove straight into the enemy's fire. I can well imagine the feelings of those tank crews when they saw an irresistible tide of vehicles and guns bearing down upon them. Trucks were still exploding in flames, but nothing could have halted that onrush, the product more of instinct than of command. The air was so heavy with dust and smoke that one could do nothing but follow the vehicle in front into the thick blanket ahead. A number of unfortunate men were thrown off motorcycles or tossed out of trucks. Their death was certain, for vehicles behind had no chance of avoiding them. . . .

My car was jammed on all sides and could not move [resumes Brigadier Kippenberger].... A few seconds later I saw the truck ahead of us turning to the left, and beyond it quite clearly saw John Gray standing with his head through the roof of his car pointing in the same direction. "We'll give it a go, Ross" [the driver], I said. "Very good, sir," he replied, as polite as ever. We followed the trucks ahead, all bolting like wild elephants. For a few moments, we ran on amid a pandemonium, overtaking and being overtaken by other frantic vehicles, dodging slit trenches, passing or crashing into running men, amid an uproar of shouts and screams. I recognized the men as Germans, pulled out my revolver and was eagerly looking out for a target when suddenly there was silence and we were running smoothly on level desert. We were through. . . .

CHAPTER 5
DECISION AT EL ALAMEIN

On August 3, 1942, Winston Churchill landed at Cairo after a one-stop flight from England in a Liberator bomber. The prime minister had decided to examine for himself what was wrong with the 8th Army and its generals. In Cairo, he saw a galaxy of top military and civilian officials from all over the Middle East. Then, wearing a pith helmet and his famous one-piece "jump suit" and clenching a long cigar in his bulldog jaw, he stumped up and down the El Alamein line in the broiling sun, talking to the troops and questioning their officers. Finally, he called for "drastic and immediate" changes in the Middle Eastern command.

Heading the list of the dismissed was General Auchinleck. Like Wavell before him, Auchinleck was tired and stained by bad luck at the moment Britain desperately needed a winner. The new Middle East commander was to be General Sir Harold Alexander, long marked for high command, handsome and distinguished, the perfect image of a general. To fill the vacant 8th Army post, Churchill selected Strafer Gott. A warm and personable man without a trace of fear, Gott had been at storm center of every fight in the desert since 1940.

Gott's record of generalship was hardly spotless, but he was without doubt the best-known and most-admired officer in the 8th Army - and after the Gazala Gallop, it became more important than ever for the men in the ranks to know and trust their commander. Ironically, the one general they had come to know above all others was the enemy's general.

The Rommel legend had grown to such epidemic proportions in the Allied camp that Auchinleck had tried to check its spread with a warning to his officers. "There exists a real danger," he wrote, "that our friend Rommel is becoming a kind of magician or bogeyman to our troops, who are talking far too much about him. . . . Even if he were a superman, it would still be highly undesirable that our men should credit him with supernatural powers. . . . We must . . . not always keep harping on Rommel." The trouble was that the desert was an empty stage; the spectacular actions of a dramatic personality like the Desert Fox were bound to impress foe as well as friend.

The men of the 8th Army knew only too well the speed and energy of Rommel's thrusts. They also knew from the stories of prisoners the hold he had over his men. They learned of his uncanny ability to be in the right place at the right time, of the charmed life he led fighting alongside the front-line troops, of the joking ways he had with the men in the ranks, and the barracks-room language he used on officers who did not measure up. (After the war, a motion picture called *The Desert Fox* was made, starring the English actor James Mason. When one of Rommel's officers was asked for his opinion of Mason's performance, he smiled and said, "Altogether too polite.") The Rommel legend flourished and gnawed at the 8th Army's morale.

The day after Churchill made his command changes, a transport plane flying Strafer Gott to Cairo was shot down by a German fighter. Gott's death symbolized the end of an era. "Only Gott remained of the original men," correspondent Alan Moorehead reported, "and he stood out like a giant. . . . He was the last of the desert rats to go."

In Gott's place was appointed Lieutenant General Bernard Montgomery, a veteran of the Battle of France in 1940 and head of the forces stationed in the south of England. On August 15, Alexander and Montgomery took up the reins of command. With their arrival, as with Rommel's arrival eighteen months before, the situation began to change.

Montgomery was fifty-five years old, small and wiry, with a long, thin nose and cold, pale blue eyes. He did not drink or smoke, and he disapproved of those who did; he had simple tastes and an "iron simplicity" of mind, with little interest in anything outside the problems of military command. Despite his austere personality, Montgomery had a remarkable flair for publicity. He deliberately set out to build himself up as the British champion; win, lose, or draw, the 8th Army would know its commander and precisely what he expected of it.

Tirelessly, Montgomery poked about the army, sizing up its commanders, bringing in new men to replace those he found wanting (especially anyone who objected to his theories), learning the peculiarities of his troops. He found, for instance, that the New Zealanders had a casual attitude toward military discipline; when he remarked to their much-decorated general, Bernard Freyberg, that they never seemed to salute, Freyberg assured him, "Wave to them, sir, and they'll wave back." From then on, Montgomery waved. Visiting the Australians, he adopted one of their wide-brimmed bush hats and decorated it with a selection of divisional badges; he also adopted a tanker's beret. Before long, a new spirit began to grow in the El Alamein lines - Monty was everywhere, Monty had taken hold, Monty was a go-getter. His stock went up further at the end of August, when he passed his first military test.

In his philosophy, Rommel drew a distinction between a bold attack and a gambling attack. Boldness in attack was always worth trying if it did not threaten the existence of the army should it fail; a gamble was called for, he wrote, only when "defeat is merely a matter of time . . . and the only chance lies in an operation of great risk." By late August 1942, he decided he must gamble.

Day by day, the Afrika Korps was falling further and further behind in the battle of supply. Ships by the dozens, filled with troops from Britain and tanks from America, were steaming around Africa bound for Egypt. The inefficient Axis supply line sputtered along, barely able to keep up with daily needs and taking nothing extra for battle. In August, it brought Rommel 13,000 tons of supplies; the 8th Army received 500,000 tons. Rommel would have to strike soon or the balance of strength tilting against him would make it impossible for him to attack at all.

On the last night of August, the Afrika Korps swept through the southern end of the British line to open the Battle of Alam el Halfa. There it stumbled into unsuspected mine fields and was delayed. The next day, as Rommel attempted to turn in behind the British, his armor was pounded hard by artillery and bombers and became enmeshed in a cunning web of defenses. Grant tanks dug in on Alam el Halfa Ridge, firing at Rommel's forces.

By September 2, the Axis offensive was stalled and in difficulty. What fuel was on hand had to be saved; of three Italian gasoline tankers on their way to Tobruk, one had been sunk and a second one damaged (it, too, was later sunk). As Rommel began to pull back, it seemed the moment for a vigorous counterattack. Montgomery, however, was content; he felt the 8th Army was not yet in any condition to drive "headlong into the enemy." He had other plans.

Each pause between battles had brought a flow of new and better weapons to the desert, and this pause was no exception. The Afrika Korps managed to increase its supply of Mark III Specials fitted with the long fifty-millimeter guns. It also received some thirty new Mark IV Specials, each mounting a powerful long-barreled seventy-five-millimeter gun; they were probably the best tanks in the desert. There were eighty-six of the eighty-eight-millimeter guns and ninety-five big antitank guns captured from the Russians that were almost as dangerous. Rommel had just over 100,000 men, half of them Italian. His main concern was how to supply them with the tools of war.

The 8th Army, meanwhile, was receiving shipload

after shipload of new tanks - American-built Shermans with seventy-five millimeter guns. Tank for tank, the Sherman was perhaps a shade inferior to the Mark IV Special, but it had an overwhelming ten-to-one superiority in numbers. The six-pounder antitank gun was now standard throughout the army, and self-propelled artillery - assault guns mounted on tank chassis - furnished additional firepower. By October, Montgomery's advantage in manpower was two to one, and in heavily gunned tanks, more than five to one. His superiority in artillery, antitank guns, and air support was also substantial.

Such figures seemed to guarantee victory for the British, except that the position at El Alamein was like nothing the two armies had seen before. In the past, there had always been an open desert flank to invite a battle of maneuver. At El Alamein, both flanks were securely anchored - on the north by the sea and on the south by the forbidding Qattara Depression, an enormous dished-out area 400 feet below sea level full of salt marshes and quicksand. Into the thirty-eight miles between these flanks, Rommel had jammed 1,600 guns, 550 tanks, 100,000 men, and 500,000 land mines. Montgomery's advantage in manpower and firepower was not too large for the kind of slugging match he expected to fight.

Operation Lightfoot, as the new British offensive was codenamed, was carefully planned to take the best advantage of 8th Army resources. The Australians, the Scottish Highlanders, and the New Zealanders were among the finest fighting troops in the world, and Montgomery built his assault around them. They were to breach the mine fields and overcome strong points, clearing a path for the armor. The tanks would then advance to form an iron shield to protect the infantry as it enveloped the remaining enemy positions, a process Montgomery called "crumbling." If Rommel counterattacked with tanks to save his infantry, the British armor would meet them defensively. Montgomery predicted the battle would last twelve days and result in complete defeat for the Afrika Korps.

Unable to maneuver in such cramped quarters, the Desert Fox set out to make the cost of victory too high for the British to pay. Among the more impervious parts of the defenses were the belts of mine fields his men called the Devil's Gardens. They averaged some five miles in depth, and scattered through them were hundreds of strong points containing machine guns, mortars, and antitank guns. Behind the mine fields was a "gun line" of dug-in artillery and heavy antitank guns. Nearby, tanks were poised to move toward any breakthrough.

Most of the mines in the Devil's Gardens were the antitank type, set to go off under the weight of a vehicle (or running man); they would destroy any truck that ran over them and cripple tanks by blowing off their tracks. Thickly sown among these large mines were thousands of small S-mines, deadly to infantry. If stepped on, a charge shot them two or three feet in the air, where they exploded. Many mines were cunningly booby-trapped so that if they were moved they set off other mines nearby. Stretched just above the ground were trip wires attached to the firing pins of 250-pound aircraft bombs. All these lethal devices were easy to plant and conceal in the desert's sandy surface.

The Desert Fox was not on hand to supervise the defenses he had planned. A year and a half of hard campaigning had left him seriously ill, and he was recalled to Germany for medical treatment in September. General Georg Stumme was sent from the Russian front to replace him. On his way home, Rommel saw both Mussolini and Hitler and complained about the supply crisis, but nothing was done. "It is sometimes a misfortune to enjoy a certain military reputation," he wrote in exasperation. "One knows one's own limits but others expect miracles."

Montgomery scheduled Operation Lightfoot to begin at night, in the light of a full moon. Four infantry divisions were to crack open the Axis line near its northern end. With the foot soldiers would go parties of sappers to search out mines, remove them, and mark safe corridors for the following armor. Nearly 900 pieces of heavy artillery would support the attack, and the RAF guaranteed control of the air. Elaborate camouflage and fleets of dummy vehicles concealed the point of attack.

Zero hour for the Battle of El Alamein was set for 9:40 on the night of October 23, 1942. At that moment, with one tremendous roar, 882 field guns loosed a rain of high explosives on the Afrika Korps. The sweating gunners rammed in shell after shell, and the gun barrels glowed with heat. Howard Kippenberger, commander of a New Zealand brigade, recalled how "the maddening incessant clamour of the guns became deafening"; for some slight shelter against the "uproar and the concussion" he and his staff crouched behind a truck. In the moonlight, the infantry could be seen moving forward at a walk, holding their rifles with fixed bayonets at the ready. Sappers advanced with them, probing for mines with bayonets and electric mine-detectors. The dew-covered tanks glistened blackly in the dazzling gun flashes. Slowly over the battlefield spread a thick, choking cloud of dust.

As the infantrymen plodded forward, they watched closely for the stalk-like prongs that marked S-mines. Here and there men were hit and fell writhing in the sand. The staccato bursts of German machine guns and the skirling of the Scottish Highlanders' bagpipes could be heard above the thunder of the barrage. In the thickening dust, attackers and defenders tangled blindly in vicious fire-fights.

Meanwhile, amidst the bullets and the shells, the sappers went about their exacting tasks. They located mines with detectors or bayonets, gingerly felt around them for trip wires and other booby traps, lifted them out and removed their detonators, and stacked them off to the side. White tapes and colored lights were put up to mark the cleared corridors. As they worked, masses of tanks and trucks and guns began to crawl forward. Many of the sappers' markers were knocked down, and vehicles blundered onto uncleared mines. By dawn, the infantry had reached most of its objectives, but the armor was still enmeshed in the Devil's Gardens.

In the Axis headquarters, all was confusion. The massive bombardment had torn up the Afrika Korps' communications links, and the forward posts could not get their information back to the high command. General Stumme set out to see for himself what was happening. Nearing the front, his car was caught by a blast of fire from Australian infantrymen. Stumme's aide was killed, and just as the general started to get out to seek cover, the driver whirled the car around to escape. As Stumme clung desperately to the side of the speeding car, he suffered a heart attack and tumbled dead to the ground. General Wilhelm Ritter von Thoma of the Afrika Korps took over command of the army. In Germany, Rommel was alerted to the British attack; that evening Hitler himself telephoned to ask him to return to North Africa.

Montgomery's brisk order for the first day of battle called for the armor to fight on through the mine fields, regardless of its losses. By dusk, the 1st Armored Division had done so, beating off counterattacks by the Afrika Korps. But that night, when the 10th Armored Division tried to carry out Montgomery's orders, it ran into an inferno of resistance.

As the division's 250 tanks and their supporting vehicles churned through the foot-deep dust in the narrow mine-field corridors, German planes lit the battlefield as brightly as day with parachute flares and dropped bombs into the tightly packed mass of transport. Ammunition and gasoline trucks blazed in one "enormous crackling furnace which lit the desert up for a radius of two miles," in the words of an eyewitness. The burning trucks became aiming points for the enemy artillery. Taking heavy losses, the 10th Armored pressed on, and by the morning of October 25, some of its units had linked up with the 1st Armored.

Montgomery finally had his armored shield for the infantry bridgehead, but no genuine breakthrough had been made. Behind the mine fields, the enemy's gun line was intact, and with daylight, it began taking a heavy toll on the British armor. A tank officer helplessly watched the Grants of his regiment "go up in sheets of flame one by one, just as if someone had lit the candles on a birthday cake," under the fire of concealed eighty-eights.

On its third day, the Battle of El Alamein was approaching a stalemate. The 8th Army had broken into the enemy's position but could get no farther; the enemy was equally frustrated when he tried to counterattack. One of Montgomery's corps commanders recalled that on October 26 "we were within an ace of losing our grip on the battle." Casualties among the attacking infantry and the sappers had been unusually heavy - the total of dead, wounded, and missing was already more than 6,100 - and exhaustion was becoming a problem. Some 300 British tanks had been knocked out, but this was no great worry - Montgomery had 800 more on call.

To retain the initiative, Montgomery decided to shift the weight of his attack to the extreme northern end of the line, near the coast road, where the Australians had taken some key ground. The infantry and armored units that had borne the brunt of the battle so far would be pulled back to rest and refit.

Rommel, who had now arrived to take over command, also made a critical decision that day. The breaching of the Devil's Gardens had removed his best chance for a "negative victory" - a stalemated battle. From now on, he thought, the Afrika Korps would be steadily ground down by superior weight. Characteristically, he chose to gamble with an armored counterattack before this weight became crushing.

That night a 300-man British detachment, most of them tough London Cockneys, took an advance post near an objective codenamed Snipe. Unknown to them, they were near the line of advance that Rommel's armor was to follow in its counterattack the next day. At first light on October 27, the Snipe detachment discovered it was in a hot spot.

Through the morning, the Cockneys pitted their nineteen antitank guns against relays of German and Italian tanks sent to dispose of them. The armor came off a poor second. Before long, more than a dozen tanks were burning or disabled. A big Mark IV Special rumbled to within thirty yards of the post before a shot from one of the six-pounders set it ablaze.

Shortly after noon, Italian tanks came perilously close to overrunning the position. Only one gun was sited to meet the attack, and it was soon out of ammunition. As three tanks closed in, a jeep carrying ammunition raced up to the silent gun, was hit, and burst into flames. The ammunition was saved, however, and gunner Charles Caliston calmly aimed and fired three times, killing all three tanks. Just as calmly, he then brewed a mug of tea on the hood of the burning jeep.

The Snipe action reached a climax late in the afternoon when the 21st Panzer Division passed by in its counterattack on the British bridgehead. Tank after tank was jolted by solid shot that glowed red as it bored through armor. Some twenty tanks and self-propelled guns were knocked out, disrupting the entire attack. That night, the survivors of Snipe withdrew with their one serviceable gun. They had destroyed thirty-seven enemy tanks and mobile guns and damaged another fifteen to twenty.

Savagely, Montgomery pressed the Australians' attacking the north, and just as savagely, the Germans resisted it. Some of Rommel's best formations, including the veteran 90th Light Division, had to be thrown into the fight. Gains were measured in yards, and the intensity of the artillery fire and the bombing surpassed anything seen before in the desert. "The situation continues very grave," Rommel wrote his wife on October 29. "By the time this letter arrives, it will no doubt have been decided whether we can hold on or not. I haven't much hope left." Two gasoline tankers he had been counting on had just been sunk at Tobruk by RAF bombers. He had used precious fuel to mass his armor and his last reserves in the north to hold Montgomery's attack, and there was little left for further maneuvering.

Frustrated in this second attempt at a breakthrough, Montgomery switched the weight of his attack once more. He believed, he told London, that Rommel "is now ripe for a real hard blow which may topple him off his perch." General Freyberg's New Zealand Division was reinforced by English and Scottish brigades to lead the way; the refitted 1st and 10th armored divisions would exploit the advance. The objective of the new assault, set for the early hours of November 2, was the final Axis gun line beyond the mine fields.

On this night, as they had on the first night of the battle, the infantry and sappers fought their way to their objectives. The artillery "storm" supporting them consumed 15,000 shells. Then came the armor, spearheaded by the 123 tanks of the 9th Armored Brigade. Its commander, Brigadier John Currie, had been told that he must break the gun line and that the army commander was willing to accept 100 percent casualties to do it.

At first light, Currie's 9th Armored Brigade charged, as the famous Light Brigade had charged at Balaklava in the Crimean War almost a century before - with the same terrible result. Twenty or so well-sited eighty-eights opened up with fearful effect. "The whole world seemed to blow up at once," remembered one of Currie's officers. The shriek of eighty-eight-millimeter high-velocity shells and the harsh clang as they struck the tanks dominated all other sounds. The armor overran and destroyed some thirty-five smaller guns, but it could not reach the eighty-eights. As the sun rose, it tinted blood-red the pillars of oily smoke from knocked-out tanks. Derelict Shermans and Grants and Crusaders were scattered thickly in every direction; one had been hit so hard that it pitched over on its side. Currie lost 103 of his tanks, a casualty rate of nearly 85 percent. The Axis gun line was bent but not broken.

Throughout the rest of the day, a fierce tank battle raged as Rommel strove to contain the two armored divisions threatening his last line of defense. Losses were heavy on both sides, but they were losses that Montgomery could afford and Rommel could not. The killing match was almost over.

On November 3, the Desert Fox began to withdraw his surviving infantry behind one of his dangerous screens of armor and antitank guns. It was a day of frustration for the 8th Army. Casualties in men and equipment had been high, and in the billowing dust and smoke, it seemed that the carnage would never end. Late in the afternoon, however, Montgomery received an unexpected helping hand from Adolf Hitler. The Führer ordered Rommel to "stand fast, yield not a yard of ground, and throw every gun and every man into the battle." There must be "no other road than that to victory or death," he warned his commander in North Africa.

So Rommel held fast and fought another day and lost his last chance for an orderly retreat. On November 4, victory came swiftly; as Montgomery had predicted, it was the twelfth day of battle. Most of the Italian infantry was without trucks and had to surrender. "The tanks came plunging through, hundreds of tanks lunging to the west through the gap . . . and wheeling north for the kill," wrote the historian of the Indian Division. The remnants of the Afrika Korps withdrew along the coast road; any units without transport had to escape on foot or surrender. Some 30,000 men gave themselves up. In a last effort to stem the tide rushing over him, Afrika Korps' General von Thoma attacked in his command tank, escaped as it went up in flames, and then stood quietly on the smoking battlefield, waiting to be taken.

Ahead of the 8th Army, wrote an eyewitness, "stretched nothing but death and destruction to the very horizon. Shattered trucks, burnt and contorted tanks, blackened and tangled heaps of wreckage not to be recognized; they scattered the landscape as thickly as stars in the sky. . . . In dugouts, pits, and trenches the dead lay tangled and piled. . . . These were details of the scene repeated again and again in every corner of the desert landscape: a great rubbish heap of metal and human flesh. So the victors sat, gazing across the gigantic desolation. . . ."

To herald the long-awaited desert victory, Winston Churchill ordered the church bells to peal from one end of Britain to the other. El Alamein, he wrote, marked "the turning of the Hinge of Fate."

CHAPTER 6
OPERATION TORCH

Less than forty-eight hours before Montgomery's thundering guns opened the Battle of El Alamein, three British commandos and five United States Army officers landed on a dark and deserted beach on the coast of French Algeria, some 2,500 miles to the west. Lying offshore in the Mediterranean was the British submarine *Seraph*, which had brought them there. As they quickly hid their canoes in a grove of trees behind the beach, American diplomat Robert Murphy appeared out of the darkness to greet them. "Welcome to North Africa," Murphy whispered. Major General Mark W. Clark, panting from his exertions, replied simply, "I'm damn glad we made it." They raked the sand smooth over their tracks and hurried to a house on a bluff overlooking the beach.

Shortly after dawn on October 22, another group of men arrived by car from the capital city of Algiers, seventy-five miles away. After exchanging greetings, the newcomers, carrying suitcases, marched into bedrooms and soon emerged wearing uniforms of the French armed forces. After a quick breakfast, everyone sat down to a long round of discussions, arguments, and exchanges of military information.

That afternoon, the owner of the house received a telephone call and shouted excitedly that the police were approaching. Since the Americans were violating the rights of a neutral nation, and the French officers were committing treason, pandemonium broke loose. Some of the Frenchmen ran for their cars after scrambling back into civilian clothes with a speed, General Clark noted, "I have seen exceeded only by professional quick-change artists." Others jumped out of windows and dashed into the woods. Clark and his aides scurried through a trap door into a dusty wine cellar.

When the police burst in a few minutes later, they found diplomat Murphy and three companions around a table littered with wine bottles, playing poker. The sudden activity at the secluded house, Murphy explained, was only "a little party." He was sure, he added, that the police would not embarrass him further by disturbing the "ladies" upstairs. After poking about, the police left.

With the talks so abruptly ended, Clark decided to

leave as soon as it was dark. The *Seraph*, which had submerged during the day, surfaced and moved to within 100 yards of the shore. But the wind had risen and breakers were crashing across the beach. When the canoes were put into the water, they immediately capsized. Stripped to their shorts, Clark and his men tried repeatedly to launch the frail craft; in the confusion, the general's pants and $2,000 in gold, brought along "for possible use in buying our way out of a jam," went to the bottom. At last, with the help of Murphy and his staff, all four canoes made it safely through the pounding surf. As dawn was breaking, the *Seraph* snatched up the bedraggled party, submerged, and headed for Gibraltar.

Clark's secret mission, full of boldness and confusion, was typical of Operation Torch. The Torch plan called for the United States, heavily supported by Britain, to invade the French North African possessions of Algeria and Morocco. In victory or defeat, Torch was sure to be spectacular. An amphibious assault from the sea is one of war's most complex operations, and the Americans were making not one but three landings. No one knew whether the troops would be greeted with bouquets or bullets; in fact, it was entirely possible that Torch would tip the balance against the Allies rather than for them.

After the fall of France in 1940, German troops had occupied only half the country and none of France's

African territories. In return, the government of Marshal Philippe Pétain at Vichy in southern France cooperated with the Nazis. Pétain, France's great hero of World War I, required all ranking French officers to honor the armistice that had ended the fighting and to swear a personal oath of loyalty to him.

This action left the officers in North Africa in a painful quandary. Military honor - which meant a great deal to a French officer - clearly required them to obey Pétain's orders to oppose an Allied attack. But it was equally clear to most of them that Nazi Germany, not the Allies, was France's mortal enemy. Their dilemma was how to uphold their honor and still serve the best interests of their country.

To further tangle an already tangled situation, many of these officers bore a grudge against their onetime ally Great Britain. Part of the reason was Britain supported General Charles de Gaulle, who had denounced the armistice and had rallied Free French forces - thus implying that any general or admiral loyal to Marshal Pétain was a traitor. But most of all, their hatred dated from July 3, 1940, when the Royal Navy attacked and severely crippled a French fleet at Oran in Algeria to prevent it from falling into German hands. Torch would have to be an all-American operation - or at least look like one.

The driving force behind Torch came from Churchill and Roosevelt. Churchill had long supported a Mediterranean grand strategy while Roosevelt was insistent that American forces join the fight against Hitler in 1942. When it became clear that the Allies were not yet strong enough to dare a frontal attack on the Germans across the English Channel, the two leaders settled on northwest Africa as the target. Their decision was made on July 25, 1942, as Auchinleck fought Rommel to a standstill at El Alamein. "Now we are on our way shoulder to shoulder," Roosevelt wrote to Churchill.

Not only would Torch deny a large part of the North African coast to the Axis, but successful landings and a rapid advance into Tunisia would trap Rommel in the Western Desert. Control of the Mediterranean sea lanes would be in Allied hands, and the entire southern flank of Europe – "the soft underbelly," as Churchill liked to call it - would be uncovered.

Set against these advantages was the chance that France would fight, perhaps routing the invaders or even going over entirely to the Axis camp. A stronger possibility was that Hitler would funnel an army into Tunisia from Sicily - only ninety miles away - and gain passage through neutral Spain for a second army to seize the Strait of Gibraltar. If this happened, the Torch forces would be trapped.

Despite all these unpleasant ifs, the war situation in the summer of 1942 demanded Allied action of the boldest kind. The road to triumph seemed to stretch ahead endlessly, and if Torch would provide a shortcut, Churchill and Roosevelt were willing to gamble on it. But it would have to be done soon. There were hints that the Germans planned to occupy French North Africa. After November, bad weather would prevent any amphibious operations until spring - probably too late. The Torch planning headquarters in London, under the command of Lieutenant General Dwight D. Eisenhower, set to work at a furious pace.

After much argument and juggling of forces, it was decided to make three simultaneous landings. Two convoys would sail from England, slip through the Strait of Gibraltar into the Mediterranean, and land at Oran and Algiers in Algeria. To guard against an enemy seizure of the strait, a third convoy would sail directly from the United States to occupy Casablanca, on the Atlantic coast of French Morocco. These moves would open an emergency lifeline to the Torch forces in the Mediterranean over the railroad connecting Casablanca and Oran. The assault troops at all three points would be American, followed ashore by the British. Until landing fields could be captured, air cover would be provided by aircraft carriers. The target date (D-day) was set for November 8, 1942.

While Eisenhower and his commanders dealt with the military details of the operation, Robert

Murphy tried to smooth the way for the invading troops. Sounding out French officers, the diplomat put together an underground network of those friendly to the Allied cause. Their role would be to take over key strong points on D-day. General Clark, Eisenhower's second in command, was a part of this secret plot.

The plotters needed to find someone besides Marshal Pétain who the French armed forces would rally to, someone who would quickly come to terms with the American invaders and get the 120,000-man French army in North Africa into the battle against the Axis. They chose General Henri Giraud, who had escaped from a German prison camp and had strong anti-Nazi opinions.

Another figure to be reckoned with was Admiral Jean Francois Darlan, head of the French Navy. Darlan had an unsavory reputation for cooperating with the Nazis, but he would probably join whichever side seemed the strongest. If the Allies won him over, he would bring the French fleet along with him. Because so many French generals and admirals opposed him, General de Gaulle was given no role in Operation Torch.

In late October, the 650 ships involved in Torch began steaming from various ports toward North Africa. Few of the thousands of soldiers, sailors, and airmen had any combat experience, and many of them were short of training as well. The last amphibious operation the United States Army had launched was in the Spanish-American War in 1898. But the risks had to be taken. "There are times in history when we cannot afford to wait for the final polish," wrote British admiral Sir Andrew Cunningham, naval commander of Torch, and in Cunningham's opinion this was one such time.

On November 5, General Eisenhower arrived at his operational headquarters at Gibraltar. He and his staff were greeted with the news of Montgomery's victory at El Alamein, and that night they watched the ships of the Algiers and Oran convoys glide through the narrow Strait of Gibraltar. Axis agents in neutral Spanish territory could not help but see the ships as well, but it was assumed that they were headed for Egypt or Malta. The German and Italian high commands laid plans to ambush them off Sicily.

By the early morning hours of November 8, the Center Task Force was in position off Oran. At 3 a.m., *Hartland* and *Walney*, onetime U.S. Coast Guard cutters turned over to the British, made a dash for the harbor to try to seize ships and port installations before the French could sabotage them. They missed the narrow entrance in the darkness; as the cutters maneuvered for another try, searchlights flicked on along the shore.

With *Walney* leading the way, the cutters charged again, smashing through two floating booms strung across the mouth of the harbor to keep out enemy submarines. By now, the defenders were fully alert. Searchlights held the two ships fast in their brilliant grip, and guns of all kinds poured out a storm of fire at them.

Nearing the spot where she was to land her assault forces, the *Walney* came under the point-blank fire of the guns of a pair of French destroyers. Torn to pieces, her decks piled high with dead and dying, *Walney* lost all power, burst into flames, and blew up. *Hartland* fared little better. Her gun crews were slaughtered, and a French destroyer pumped shell after shell into her at a range of 100 feet. The survivors abandoned ship as the burning cutter drifted aimlessly with the tide.

Despite this disastrous beginning, the Oran operation went like clockwork. The 39,000 assault troops streamed ashore on beaches some twenty miles east and west of the city. The French were surprised, but their opposition was sharp despite the abundance of American flags carried by the invaders. Fighting continued that day and the next as the Americans consolidated their beachheads and closed in on Oran. On the morning of November 10, the city surrendered.

At Algiers, meanwhile, the action had been more political than military. At three landing beaches flanking the city, the British and American troops came ashore against scarcely any opposition at all. As the landing forces began moving on Algiers itself, the city was in an advanced state of confusion. Murphy's underground plotters had gone into action. Bands of young rebels armed with a rag-tag of weapons seized the radio station, the central telephone switchboard, police stations, and even some military headquarters. By two on the morning of D-day, as scheduled, the plotters were ready to hand Algiers over to the Americans without a drop of blood being shed. But no Americans appeared. They were ten or fifteen miles away. What the underground had not been told, because of the need for secrecy, was that the landings would take place on beaches well to the east and west of the city.

With infinite pains, one observer noted, Robert Murphy "had assembled a nicely filled apple cart"; now the American diplomat was trying to keep it from being kicked over. As the rebels ranged the city, Murphy hurried to the home of the French North African army commander, General Alphonse Juin. General Juin sympathized with the Allies, but he could not declare a ceasefire without the approval of his superior, Admiral Darlan, who had unexpectedly appeared in Algiers. Juin telephoned Darlan and asked him to join them right away.

It was not yet 2 a.m. when Darlan arrived. As Murphy told him of Operation Torch, Darlan exploded at what he called an unprovoked attack. While the short, stocky admiral angrily paced back and forth, the tall American diplomat paced alongside him, trying to match his steps to the short strides of the Frenchman and pleading with him to "strike an effective blow now for the liberation of France" by declaring a ceasefire. But Darlan had decided on a waiting game, to see if the Americans were really arriving in the strength that Murphy claimed. With the excuse that he would have to get in touch with Marshal Pétain, the admiral began to stall.

At dawn on D-day, the Vichy radio began to broadcast over and over Marshal Pétain's statement – "We are attacked. We shall defend ourselves. That is the order I am giving." Vichy police and military units set about reclaiming the key points in Algiers and hauling the rebels away to jail. Police arrived at General Juin's home, overpowered the rebels that surrounded it, and put Murphy under arrest.

After a final dizzy whirl, the situation in Algiers was stabilized. One of the rebels managed to reach General Charles Ryder, commander of the American landing forces, and pleaded with him to abandon the methodical, carefully planned encirclement of the city. Algiers was Ryder's for the taking, the Frenchman said – "but by noon it will be too late." Ryder ordered a swift, direct advance, and late that afternoon, a local ceasefire was arranged. At dusk on November 8, the Allies held Algiers.

Admiral Darlan, however, was not willing to quit his slippery game just yet. He refused to order an armistice for all French North Africa, nor would he command French forces in Tunisia to stop German troops from landing there. His hand was strengthened when General Giraud, the "big name" Murphy had been counting on, arrived the next day in Algiers. It turned out that Giraud had no support at all, and he was ignored by everyone but the Americans. Only Darlan seemed to have the power of decision, and Darlan was going to wait a bit longer to see which way to jump. As a result, several hundred Americans and Frenchmen died unnecessarily at Casablanca and Oran.

The assault on Casablanca was the biggest gamble of all, for the Atlantic coastal waters were seldom calm that late in the year. As the Western Task Force approached the Moroccan coast, weather forecasters in Washington and London predicted a storm and a fifteen-foot surf on November 8, too high for landing craft. But the task force's own weatherman insisted that the storm would pass. The advice of the man on the spot was taken, and by the early hours of D-day, as the ships took position off Casablanca, the Atlantic was as calm as a millpond. The assault troops waited nervously, with only a few lights and the smell of charcoal smoke indicating that land was nearby. "Africa was never so dark and mysterious to ancient sea rovers as she seemed that night to these seventy thousand young men," wrote an eyewitness, historian Samuel Eliot Morison.

The Casablanca landings, like those at Algiers and Oran, were made at beaches flanking the city. The main force, landing at a fishing village called Fedala, fifteen miles north of Casablanca, met little resistance. Its chief troubles came from batteries of coastal defense guns firing at the ships offshore, but before long, American cruisers and destroyers had silenced them. The light cruiser *Brooklyn* rained 757 shells from her six-inch guns on one coastal battery in a little more than an hour.

At Safi, well to the south of Casablanca, the landing operation was as smooth as silk. It was decided to attack the port head-on, the old destroyers *Bernadou* and *Cole* leading the way with loads of specially trained assault troops. Their sudden arrival out of the darkness triggered a blast of gunfire from the defenders, but the destroyers returned the fire with such accuracy that they all but silenced the entire harbor defense system. Before the day was far along, Safi was firmly under control, Sherman tanks were put ashore on the wharves, and the army could count only twenty-nine casualties in the landing.

The northernmost landing at Port Lyautey, by contrast, was the most fiercely contested of any in Operation Torch. Landing operations got into a fearful tangle, with landing craft coming ashore late, at the wrong places, and then being wrecked as they grounded. The defenses were well handled, and reinforcements were close by. For a time, the invaders were in a critical situation, but finally they began to gain the upper hand. Carrier planes helped break up a counterattack by French tanks, and the battleship *Texas* reached seven miles inland with its main battery of fourteen-inch guns to shatter a truck convoy full of reinforcements. Yet it took four days of hard fighting and cost close to 400 American casualties before Port Lyautey's stubborn defenders were overwhelmed.

While the three landing forces flanking the city were consolidating their beachheads on D-day, a savage naval battle was raging off Casablanca itself. This was a tragic and unnecessary action, the bitter fruit of Admiral Darlan's little game; hearing nothing to the contrary from Darlan, Admiral François Michelier at Casablanca obeyed Pétain's orders to fight.

Michelier had eleven submarines, nine destroyers, and a light cruiser ready for sea, backed up by several batteries of coast-defense guns and the unfinished battleship *Jean Bart*, unable to sail but with her fifteen-inch guns operational. To guard against any French naval action and to screen the landing operations at nearby Fedala, American admiral Kent Hewitt had the new battleship *Massachusetts*, one light and three heavy cruisers, and more than a dozen destroyers, plus planes from the fleet carrier *Ranger* and a small escort carrier.

The problem of the *Jean Bart* was quickly solved. The French battleship opened fire on the *Massachusetts* at 7 a.m., narrowly missing the big battlewagon, which replied immediately. Within twenty minutes, five of her massive sixteen-inch shells had hit the *Jean Bart*, one of them putting the main battery out of action. The American warships had less luck silencing the pesky shore batteries.

An hour later, Admiral Michelier ordered seven of his destroyers and the light cruiser *Primauguet* to strike the troop transports and landing craft off Fedala. A black-robed priest stood on the breakwater, blessing the doomed ships as they steamed past. Admiral Hewitt's warships converged to meet them. For an hour and a half, the outgunned French made skillful use of smoke screens and maneuvered radically to avoid the hail of shells splashing around them.

Their good luck could not last forever. A salvo from the *Massachusetts* and one from the heavy cruiser *Tuscaloosa* hit a French destroyer at the same time and blew her to pieces. The light cruiser *Brooklyn* sent another destroyer to the bottom, and along with the heavy cruiser *Augusta*, mangled the *Primauguet*, killing two thirds of her crew. Fighter planes from the *Ranger* caused heavy casualties by strafing the French ships. By noon, the gallant sortie of Michelier's squadron was over. Two of his ships were sunk, a third was dead in the water, abandoned and burning, and four other cripples had limped back to Casablanca and beached themselves in the harbor. All of the eighteen or so torpedoes fired by French submarines in the engagement missed; the American force took five minor hits by naval or shore guns and lost one landing craft.

On November 10, General Mark Clark confronted Admiral Darlan in Algiers. Towering menacingly over the little admiral, Clark told him bluntly that he had the choice of ordering a ceasefire throughout North Africa or going to prison - and he had thirty minutes to make up his mind. Darlan gave the necessary orders, and the next day the fighting at Casablanca ended.

The ceasefire marked the end of Operation Torch. If it created more political problems than it solved, as a military operation it was a brilliant success - a fact the enemy realized only too well. On D-day, as news poured in of the landings at Casablanca, Oran, and Algiers, a German staff officer stationed in Morocco exclaimed to a French official: "This is the greatest setback to German arms since 1918.

The Americans will take Rommel in the rear, and we shall be expelled from Africa." As he said it, the Frenchman noted, tears rolled down his cheeks.

CHAPTER 7
MASTERS OF NORTH AFRICA

If the tide of World War II can be said to have turned at any one point in time, that point occurred in November 1942. In the foul jungles of Guadalcanal, as the last Japanese counterattack was hurled back, the United States took a permanent grip on the initiative in the Pacific. In Russia, the ferocious struggle for Stalingrad turned against Hitler as the Red Army encircled 300,000 German troops. And in North Africa, the twin successes of El Alamein and Operation Torch opened wide the gates of opportunity to the Allies.

This opportunity for quick, complete victory in North Africa had to be grasped immediately, however. The first chance came along the coast road west of El Alamein, as Rommel's beaten troops fled before the victorious 8th Army. If Montgomery could throw an armored flanking column across the road ahead of the remnants of the Panzerarmee, the job begun at such cost at El Alamein would be finished in one stroke.

Montgomery's painstaking battle plan had included a force to pursue the beaten enemy - Montgomery never doubted that the enemy would be beaten - but the three divisions he named a *corps de chasse* were sucked into the battle and badly mauled. At the very moment of victory, he had to improvise a new *corps de chasse*, one that was neither stocked with extra fuel nor rested and fresh for the chase.

"The essence of an armoured pursuit," wrote a historian of the campaign, "is speed and boldness to the point of fool-hardiness." Such a pursuit was, in fact, a perfect example of Rommel's theory of boldness - a driving, headlong rush with much to gain and no real threat to the army if it failed. But this was not Bernard Montgomery's way. He was a master of the set-piece engagement, superbly skilled at planning and preparing an army for battle and in balancing and adjusting forces on the battlefield. It was against his nature to take military risks, to indulge in what he called "mad rush" tactics. Nor, perhaps, was the Rommel legend quite dead. Even in defeat the Desert Fox's reputation inspired caution among his pursuers.

The result was a series of frustrating near-misses. At first the very size of the 8th Army was a handicap, and the monumental traffic jam that developed as the *corps de chasse* tried to shake free cost some twelve hours. One trap misfired when a British column cut in toward the coast road too soon; another failed when the pursuers stopped for the night while their quarry kept moving. The New Zealanders were held up half a day by a mine field that turned out not only to be a dummy, but a dummy laid by the British themselves during the Gazala Gallop.

Most frustrating of all was the plight of the 1st Armored Division, which made a long dash through the desert toward Matruh - the site of Rommel's dazzling victory the previous June - only to run out of gasoline twice and lose the race. On the evening of November 6, with Rommel's hopes for escape already growing brighter, the heavens opened wide and rain deluged the two armies. On the desert tracks, the *corps de chasse* was immediately axle-deep in mud. On the paved coast road, the Panzerarmee limped on in the rain - and was finally out of reach.

So one Allied opportunity was lost, but another soon appeared in its place - Tunisia. By quickly seizing and holding this very defensible country, the Torch army could sever Rommel's supply line and leave him hopelessly trapped. Tunisia, in fact, had once been on the list of Torch's D-day objectives, but with all the other uncertainties, it seemed too much of a gamble to attempt an amphibious landing under the very nose of the Axis air force in Sicily. Still, the need to strike fast for Tunisia never left Eisenhower's thoughts. "This single objective was constantly held before all eyes," he wrote.

There were some 15,000 French troops in Tunisia, poorly armed but strong enough to deny the country to the Axis at least temporarily - if they would fight. Admiral Darlan, however, shrank from ordering the Tunisian garrison to shoot at Germans, even after ordering the shooting at the Allies in Algeria and Morocco to stop. Nor could the French commanders of the garrison bring themselves to put aside notions of military honor and loyalty to Marshal Pétain to act on their own.

As the hours slipped away and General Clark tried to pin down the squirming Darlan, the Germans scraped up men and guns and hurled them across the Sicilian narrows. French units sat in their weapons pits around the Tunisian airfields and watched impassively as scores of Junkers transport planes spiraled down and landed. Soon a thin line of German troops held the primary northern ports of Tunis and Bizerte and the defensive ground around them and began to trickle southward to "hold the door open" for Rommel.

(It took months to straighten out the troublesome

political tangle centered in Algiers. The uproar in the United States and Britain over the so-called Darlan Deal ended only when Darlan was assassinated on Christmas Eve of 1942 by a young French patriot. General Giraud then took over, but he proved to be, in President Roosevelt's tart phrase, "a very slender reed" to depend upon. Finally, General de Gaulle brought order out of the confusion. Free French forces were rearmed and eventually played an important role in liberating their homeland from Nazi rule.)

The door of opportunity was still ajar, for the German beachhead was very weak, and the Allies were racing hard for Tunis. More than 550 miles of rugged, mountainous country lay before them. "Get there somehow, and get there quick" was their motto, a war correspondent wrote. "No one quite knew what enemy, if any, was ahead or to the flanks, but morale was up to the limits and there was an infectious air of excitement. . . ." Infantrymen and paratroopers, U.S. Rangers and British commandos, rushed on, never knowing if there would be fuel or ammunition - or food - for the next day.

By mid-November, the Allies were well across the Tunisian border but facing stiffening resistance. The Axis poured men into Tunisia at the rate of more than 1,000 a day, a pace the Allies could not match. The Luftwaffe harassed the advancing columns. Nevertheless, a British force pushed to within a dozen miles of Tunis before it was forced back. The race was in its last lap, the outcome was hanging in the balance - and then the rains came.

The soil of northern Tunisia has a peculiar consistency, and overnight it turned into one great soft sea of mud. "Tunisian mire has a flypaper quality all its own," wrote Hollywood producer Darryl Zanuck, a colonel in the Signal Corps. "There are no puddles and you don't slip or splash; you just sink in sort of gentle-like and stay there." General Eisenhower toured the front before a major attack he had scheduled for Christmas Eve. Everywhere he looked the army was bogged down; at one point he watched as four soldiers tried to get a single motorcycle out of a mud hole, became swamped themselves, and finally left the machine mired deeper than when they began. Bitterly disappointed, he called off the attack. The race for Tunis was over.

The stalemate in Tunisia during the winter of 1942–43, like the siege of Tobruk in 1941, was bloody and monotonous and frustrating; only but instead of the heat and dust of Tobruk, the troops in Tunisia lived in cold and mud. It was a winter full of those little incidents of war that seemed especially senseless when neither side could gain an advantage. Correspondent Alan Moorehead recorded one such incident, in a village called El Aroussa, in January, 1943.

"The morning broke unusually clear, and I wandered into the village," Moorehead wrote. "In the main street half a dozen Tommies were washing in the horse trough, and I fell into conversation with them. They were Londoners, adolescent boys on their first campaign and enjoying a good deal of it. Their backs and chests as they washed were very white, but their faces had gone scarlet through exposure. . . . They were friendly and shy and very determined to do well in the war. . . .

"As I walked back to my camp the Stukas came over. . . . It seemed for a moment that they were going to sail by the village, but at the last moment they altered direction, opened their flaps, and dived. The bombs tumbled out lazily, turning over and over in the morning sunshine. Then with that graceful little jump and a flick, each aircraft turned upward and out of its dive and wheeled away. . . .

"I walked over to the centre of the village, keeping care to stay away from an exploding ammunition lorry. A barnlike building had taken a direct hit, and the coiled barbed wire [stored there] had threshed about wildly in a thousand murderous tentacles. The blast had carried these fragments across to the water trough, and now my six young friends were curiously huddled up and twisted over one another. It is the stillness of the dead that is so shocking. Even their boots don't seem to lie on the ground as those of a sleeping man would. They don't move at all. They seem to slump into the earth with such unnatural overwhelming tiredness. . . ."

In the desert to the east, meanwhile, the retreat of the Panzerarmee continued. The British pursued doggedly, relentlessly, unable to catch up to Rommel but giving him no rest either. On November 23, for the third time in less than two years, he was back at El Agheila. There the Panzerarmee held for three weeks, gravely wounded but still dangerous, while Montgomery stock-piled supplies for an attack. On December 13, as the British barrage began, the Desert Fox pulled out.

After another three-week pause at Buerat, some 200 miles to the west, the retreat continued. Tripoli could not be defended, and on January 23, 1943, the 8th Army marched into the city. Since the days of Wavell and O'Connor, British soldiers had dreamed of taking Tripoli, seemingly as unreachable as a desert mirage. Now, wrote a correspondent, they "stood with wonderment and emotion beside the playing fountains" - and then marched on westward. On February 12, the second anniversary of Rommel's arrival in North Africa, the rear guards of the Afrika Korps withdrew across the Libyan border into Tunisia. The Axis dug in at the formidable Mareth Line.

This kind of retreat had gone against all Rommel's instincts. His orders had been to withdraw as slowly as possible, holding off the 8th Army as long as possible. Rommel favored either withdrawal from North Africa (given Axis supply problems, he believed the campaign was a lost cause) or the classic strategy of an army threatened with entrapment: rapid concentration to defeat the enemy forces in detail before they could combine against him. Every mile Rommel retreated shortened his supply line and lengthened the 8th Army's, allowing him to retreat a great deal faster than the British could chase him. The Desert Fox had wanted to hurry to Tunisia, connect with General Hans-Jürgen von Arnim's 5th Panzer Army there to rout the still-weak Torch army, and then turn on the 8th Army while it dangled at the end of its long supply line.

He flew to Germany to raise these matters of strategy with Hitler. The reaction was, in Rommel's words, "like a spark in a powder barrel. The Führer flew into a fury. . . . I began to realize that Adolf Hitler simply did not want to see the situation as it was and that he reacted emotionally against what his intelligence must have told him was right."

Rommel was still determined to seize the initiative if he could. In February 1943, leaving his infantry in the Mareth Line to hold off Montgomery, he led the Afrika Korps northward for an assault on the Americans in the narrow "waist" of Tunisia. On February 14, the panzers sprang forward to the attack.

Suddenly it was the old glory days all over

again - the quick surprise thrust, the reeling enemy, the Desert Fox leading from up front, the waves of consternation spreading through the opposing high command like ripples through a pond after the splash of a stone. Two panzer columns ripped through the thin American line, converged on a mountain gap called Kasserine Pass, brushed aside the force defending it, and poured through the pass into the American rear areas. Desperate counterattacks were methodically chewed up by German tanks and antitank guns.

Collecting every unit they could lay hands on, the Allied commanders labored to plug the gap. Early in the Kasserine battle the green U.S. troops and their inexperienced commanders had been badly knocked about by Rommel's desert veterans; now they began to dig in their heels stubbornly, particularly hard-fighting units of the U.S. 1st Armored Division. "They recovered very quickly after the first shock," Rommel wrote. On February 22, unable to achieve a breakthrough, he pulled back through Kasserine Pass.

Two weeks later, Rommel tried a second attack, this time against the 8th Army near Mareth. But the old magic was gone. He was exhausted mentally and sick physically, and he mishandled the attack. His armor charged blindly and was cut to pieces by Montgomery's antitank guns; some fifty tanks were lost, while the British lost but half a dozen.

On March 9, 1943, his health broken, the Desert Fox left North Africa, never to return.

By the end of March, the Torch army's losses at Kasserine Pass had been made good. Units were consolidated and inept commanders weeded out, and General Alexander arrived from Cairo to command the Allied ground forces. It was now a battle against time, a battle to end the campaign in Tunisia in time to assault Sicily and Italy that summer. If von Arnim could hold out for three or four months, however, no further Allied campaigns would be possible in 1943. This would suit Hitler very well indeed, giving him the chance to concentrate all his forces for one last mighty thrust at Russia.

The terrain facing the 8th Army in southern Tunisia was on the familiar desert pattern, but the rugged, mountainous north was something else entirely. In desert fighting, the armies were spread out and concealed in dust clouds, and the progress of a battle was seldom easy to follow. In northern Tunisia, on the other hand, it was usually possible to see the enemy positions clearly and to plot the course of the battle without difficulty. In the sector manned by the British 1st Army, for example, there was a long and bitter struggle for a piece of high ground known as Longstop Hill. The climactic British assault on Longstop, made in late April, looked like this to an eyewitness:

"Everything appeared to happen in miniature. The

tanks climbing on Jebel Ang looked like toys. The infantry that crept across the uplands toward [the village of] Heidous were tiny dark dots, and when the mortar shells fell among them it was like drops of rain on a muddy puddle. Toy donkeys toiled up the tracks toward the mountain crests, and the Germans, too, were like toys, little animated figures that occasionally got up and ran or bobbed up out of holes in the ground between the shell explosions."

As Longstop was being overrun, another equally bitter battle was being fought for Hill 609 in the American sector a few miles to the north. This high ground - named for its height in meters on the maps the Allies were using - was blocking the advance of the American 2nd Corps, commanded by Major General Omar Bradley. For four days, the fight for Hill 609 raged. Von Arnim's stubborn infantrymen were dug into cracks and crevices on the stony heights, and their mortars and artillery dominated all the approaches to the hill.

"Seldom has an enemy contested a position more bitterly than did the Germans high on Hill 609," wrote General Bradley. They rolled hand grenades down on the Americans clawing for a foothold on the steep slopes, and their strong points were taken only after hand-to-hand combat with pistols, knives, and fists. Each American gain was met by a vicious counterattack. Finally, Bradley ordered Sherman tanks forward to provide fire support. They nosed up to the foot of the hill and chipped away at the enemy positions with their seventy-five millimeter guns, their armor proof against the bullets and grenades showered down on them.

At last, on May 1, Hill 609 was encircled and the defenders hunted down. The capture was sweet revenge for the U.S. 34th Infantry Division. The 34th had been badly mauled by the Afrika Korps at Kasserine Pass in February, losing both its reputation and its self-respect in the process. Now it regained both, with interest.

Already, Montgomery, in a masterful display of battlefield tactics, had forced the Mareth Line and linked up with the Torch army. The loss of Longstop and Hill 609, combined with heavy pressure from the 8th Army, drove von Arnim back to his final line of defense overlooking the approaches to Tunis and Bizerte. Last-minute attempts to fly in reinforcements from Sicily met with disaster. Scores of Junkers transports and mammoth six-engined Messerschmitt troop carriers were knocked into the sea by Allied fighters.

On May 6, behind a tremendous artillery barrage and a bombing attack, the last German line was blown open. Tanks burst through like water through a broken dam. "In scores, in hundreds, this vast procession of steel lizards went grumbling and lurching and swaying up the Tunis road," wrote correspondent Moorehead. The next day, Tunis itself was in sight. It was especially fitting that the Desert Rats of the British 7th Armored Division, their famous red jerboa emblem still decorating their vehicles, were among the first to enter the city. The Desert Rats were bringing to an end the long campaign they had begun under O'Connor in those far-off days of 1940.

That same day, the Americans reached Bizerte. A force of Grant tanks swept into the city, exchanging fire with snipers and the German rear guard. A crewman of one of the tanks described the scene in a letter to his family.

"By this time it was getting very hot and stuffy in the tank," he wrote, "so we climbed out and took a smoke. . . . Then a Frenchman comes up with a bottle of wine and we all had a smoke and drank the bottle of wine. A shell lands behind the tank and sort of makes us mad, so we get back in and start shooting away again - and the people just standing there on the sidewalk. Every time George would shoot the seventy-five, plaster would fall down from all the buildings around, but they didn't seem to mind that, they were so glad to see us. . . ."

Axis troops were now surrendering in droves. Many tried to flee to Cape Bon, a finger of land jutting out into the Mediterranean, but when they saw that there were no ships or planes to carry them across to Sicily, they too gave themselves up. As the men of his Afrika Korps marched into captivity, Rommel was with Hitler in Berlin. "I should have listened to you before," the dejected Führer told him, "but I suppose it's too late now. It will soon be all over in Tunisia."

It was all over on May 13, 1943. Close to 275,000 Axis troops were captured in the last week of battle. They stacked their weapons and came into Allied lines in endless, orderly columns of trucks. Almost none escaped. "It is my duty to report that the Tunisian campaign is over," General Alexander cabled Prime Minister Churchill. "All enemy resistance has ceased. We are the masters of the North African shores."

The crushing defeat in North Africa was the beginning of the end for the Axis partners. Before the year was out, Sicily and Italy were invaded, and massive Russian attacks rolled back the Germans on the eastern front. In June 1944, the Allies attacked across the English Channel to win a foothold on the Normandy shores; by fall, France was liberated and the battle for Germany had begun.

For some, North Africa was the first step on the road to military fame. Eisenhower became supreme commander of Allied forces in Europe, with Montgomery the head of his ground forces. Alexander commanded the forces in the Mediterranean theater. American generals such as Bradley, bloodied in Tunisia, went on to carve important niches for themselves in the European campaign. But for others the desert war was the climax of their military careers. Wavell and Auchinleck, for example, later served in relative obscurity in the Far East; General Ritchie ended up as a corps commander in Europe under Montgomery.

For Erwin Rommel, who put such a unique, personal stamp on the desert war, the future brought only disillusionment and doom. In July 1944, while commanding the German forces in Normandy, he was gravely wounded in an air attack. A few days later, a group of generals, convinced that Hitler was insane and dragging Germany down to destruction in a war already lost, tried to kill the Führer by planting a bomb in his headquarters. Rommel, who had long since come to despise Hitler, knew of the plot to overthrow him but took no part in it. Nor did he know that the conspirators planned to name him head of state to negotiate peace if they succeeded. But Hitler survived, and in the purge that followed, Rommel was implicated.

He was at his home recovering from his wounds when Hitler's police came. They gave him the choice of suicide by poison or a public execution, with its disgrace to his family and his memory. He chose to kill himself. His son, Manfred, saw the body soon afterward. "My father lay on a camp bed in his brown Africa uniform," he said, "a look of contempt on his face." The German people were told that the Desert Fox had died of the wounds suffered in Normandy, and on October 18, 1944, he was given a hero's funeral. Seven months later, Hitler also killed himself, and Germany lay defeated and in ruins.

Incident at Kasserine Pass

As Rommel's surprise thrust closed in on the American units guarding Kasserine Pass, a reconnaissance unit of the Afrika Korps slipped behind the American lines to seize a small bridge beyond the pass. Its commander, Captain Heinz Schmidt, told of his experience in his book *With Rommel in the Desert*.

> Swiftly I mustered an assault platoon of three officers and 21 men armed with automatic weapons. With as much ammunition as we could carry, we crawled through the cover of the undergrowth towards the nearest gully. . . . Our luck held. The gully ran right into the wadi which the bridge crossed. It was not much of a bridge, a little above six feet high and perhaps twelve feet long.
>
> I had two machine guns positioned on either side of the approach to the wadi and the bridge, facing in the direction of the enemy's rear. Darkness dropped suddenly on the valley. And then within minutes, a vehicle approached from the enemy region.

As it roiled towards the bridge we tried to hold it up. The truck slowed down, but the men in it recognized us as Germans. One of them fired at us. The truck accelerated and thrashed its way across the bridge before we could recover from our surprise.

That was a lesson. We were wiser when the next vehicle was heard rumbling towards us and loomed up in vague shape in the thickening darkness. The truck came on fast. Both my machine guns let rip at it from either side of the road. The truck swerved off the road and capsized. One of my men leaped up and made prisoners of the men in it - four men, two of them wounded. . . .

A few minutes later six American riflemen were crossing the bridge. They were almost in the middle of it when they were taken with a gasp. Within seconds, we heard the sound of another truck approaching. We leaped for cover, and as the truck approached the bridge we turned the machine guns on it. This time our prisoners included three officers. . . .

With the two shot-up trucks, I had my men rapidly improvise a road block on the bridge.

Several more American trucks ran up to the road block, slowed down, stopped - and we took the men in them without firing a shot. . . .

One of the prisoners was a lieutenant, a breezy character. We chatted away in a strangely cheerful way under that Kasserine bridge about our private affairs. He came from Brooklyn, he said. He lived there with his wife and two children. "A magnificent city," I managed in my broken English. "I should like to see it some day."

"That," he said half-mockingly, "can probably be arranged soon." I got his meaning, and side-stepped: "I think it's going to take us some time to win the war." We both laughed. . . .

Half an hour had passed since the last truck had run into our road block. Now I heard a droning in the distance to the north. The ground began to tremble slightly. Suspicious, I climbed from the wadi to the top of the bank. In the open air, the sound of motors purred clearly from where we knew the Americans lay. Enemy tanks, undoubtedly. "If tanks advance on the bridge," I ordered the nearest machine gun, "do not shoot - let them cross." The drone of the engines and the clank of the tracks grew louder. A tank loomed up on the road, appearing colossal against the background of the starry heavens.

The hatch was open, and the commander was standing exposed and looking around. The tank pulled up. "Why this barricade?" his voice rang out. He got no reply. My men had pistols in the ribs of the prisoners below the bridge. The tank commander spoke swiftly to his driver. The tank thrust on, heaving the wrecked trucks to one side.

And then one of our machine guns let rip directly at the tank turret! I had forgotten to ensure that my order reached the gun on the far side of the wadi. Like a rabbit at his hole, the commander dropped down into his turret. The tank sprayed out fire wildly. Thundering, it rolled over the bridge above our heads. The droning went on, and then the rumbling thunder again, the squeak and rattle of tracks.

Another tank passed over the bridge, another and another, one more, then the fifth and last. . . .

The next hour was tense. The American lieutenant from Brooklyn offered me some chewing gum and a cigarette. I seldom smoked, but I felt that a cigarette might do me good. The possibility that I might see Brooklyn, or at least some part of

America, before the end of hostilities no longer seemed so remote. . . . I could feel the lieutenant watching me intently. I put on my calmest face. "I'll send out a patrol," I thought, "and if the tanks have definitely pulled off, I must get back. . . ."

"Well, what's happening, bud?" The American lieutenant had moved closer. I shrugged my shoulders indifferently and replied shortly, "Wait!" We dropped into our rather aimless personal conversation again. It was an odd situation. Neither American nor German knew who would be the prisoner next morning. . . .

Then again the droning of tanks, this time from Kasserine. Some distance away the returning tanks opened fire on the bridge. Their cannon shells whammed past and into the bank. Again the shaking of the earth under our feet, the clank and grumble of the tracks, the thunder on the bridge overhead. The tanks went over and on. My machine gunners scrambled back to their positions. The drone of tank engines faded in the distance, like tuneless bagpipes.

The Americans and I looked at each other again. The lieutenant from Brooklyn grinned. "Have some gum, bud," he said. . . .

The men got ready. I turned to the small group of officers, and in my indifferent English told them: "Gentlemen, one of you, together with an ambulance man, may remain with the wounded." I left it to them to decide which of them was to stay behind. They did it swiftly, tossing a coin, heads or tails, eliminating. The final toss lay between a captain and the lieutenant from Brooklyn. Now I was interested too. The coin spun in the darkness again and dropped to the earth. Heads! The lieutenant had called heads. He was to stay. He was not to be my prisoner, and I was glad of it. . . .

As we left the bridge the lieutenant called out in a whisper: "Good-by, bud - see ya in Berlin!" His mockery was not unpleasant. I called softly: "Auf Wiedersehen - in Brooklyn, when the war is over."

Printed in Great
Britain
by Amazon